Everything All Through All At The Same Time

By

Alwy M. Jones

Alwy M. Jones

Buy Me Coffee

Telegram

WhatsApp

YouTube

Alwy M. Jones

Copyright © 2024 Alwy Jones
All Rights Reserved

Alwy M. Jones

> We are not makers of history. We are made by history.
>
> **Martin Luther King, Jr.**

Alwy M. Jones

Unveiling the Epic Saga of Humankind

From the first flickering flames of civilization to the pulsing digital heartbeat of our modern world, human history is an epic tale of triumph and tragedy, innovation and destruction, courage and folly. This book invites you on an extraordinary journey through time, uncovering the hidden connections that bind us to our ancestors and shape our future.

Imagine standing amid the dust and clamor of ancient Mesopotamia as the first cities rise from the fertile crescent, witnessing the birth of writing and the dawn of recorded history. Fast forward to the windswept plains of Giza, where colossal pyramids scrape the sky, testaments to human ingenuity and the eternal quest for immortality.

But history is more than a parade of grand events and larger-than-life figures. It's the story of countless individuals whose names may be lost to time, but whose collective actions have shaped our world. It's the tale of ideas that have changed the course of nations, of inventions that have revolutionized daily life, and of movements that have challenged injustice and expanded the boundaries of human rights.

In these pages, you'll encounter visionaries and tyrants, inventors and artists, rebels and peacemakers. You'll uncover the hidden stories behind familiar events, and discover turning points you never knew existed. From the Silk Road to the Information Superhighway, from the Gutenberg press to the smartphone in your pocket, you'll trace the intricate web of cause and effect that connects past to present.

As you delve into this rich tapestry of human experience, you'll gain not just knowledge, but understanding. You'll see how the challenges we face today echo those of our ancestors, and how the lessons of history can illuminate our path forward. You'll discover that the past is not a dry collection of dates and facts, but a living, breathing entity that continues to shape our world in profound ways.

Alwy M. Jones

Unraveling the Complexities of Himba Hospitality

In the arid landscapes of northern Namibia, the Himba people have preserved a cultural practice that challenges Western notions of marriage, hospitality, and gender roles. Known as Okujepisa Omukazendu, which loosely translates to "offering a wife to a guest," this tradition has both fascinated and perplexed outsiders for generations.

Okujepisa Omukazendu dates back centuries and is deeply rooted in the Himba's nomadic past. In a harsh environment where survival often depended on cooperation and goodwill between clans, this practice served as a way to strengthen social bonds and ensure hospitality.

The tradition involves a married man offering his wife to a male guest for the night. However, it's crucial to understand that this practice is far more nuanced than it might initially appear to outsiders.

Contrary to common misconceptions, Okujepisa Omukazendu is not a free for all or a sign of female subjugation. Women have agency in this practice. They can refuse if they wish, and their husbands are expected to respect this decision. Moreover, the practice is governed by strict social rules. It's typically reserved for honored guests or visiting friends from other villages. There's a strong emphasis on discretion and respect for all parties involved.

The role of women in Himba society is complex. While the practice might seem patriarchal to outsiders, Himba women often hold significant power within their communities. They own the family's livestock and have a say in major decisions.

Okujepisa Omukazendu serves several social functions beyond mere hospitality. It's a way of strengthening ties between families and clans. Children born from these encounters are considered legitimate and are fully integrated into the community. This practice also plays a role in conflict resolution. In some cases, it's used to settle disputes between men or to reconcile after a conflict.

As with many traditional practices, Okujepisa Omukazendu faces challenges in the modern world. Many young Himba, especially those who have been exposed to urban life are questioning this tradition. There's a growing debate within the community about its place in modern Himba society.

The HIV/AIDS epidemic has also forced a reevaluation of the practice. Health workers have raised concerns about the potential for disease transmission, leading some Himba to modify or abandon the tradition.

Okujepisa Omukazendu has often been misunderstood and sensationalized by outside observers. It's crucial to avoid viewing this practice through a Western lens. What might seem shocking or immoral to outsiders is a normalized and respected tradition within Himba culture.

However, the practice has also faced criticism from within. Some Himba women's rights activists argue that it reinforces patriarchal control over women's bodies, despite the element of female choice.

Understanding Okujepisa Omukazendu offers valuable insights into the complexity of human cultures. This tradition challenges our assumptions about universal norms in marriage, sexuality, and hospitality. It reminds us that human societies have developed diverse ways of structuring relationships and social bonds. For the Himba, the practice is intertwined with their worldview and values. It's not just about sex or hospitality. It's about trust, community, and our understanding of what it means to be truly welcoming.

As the Himba navigate the pressures of modernization, the future of Okujepisa Omukazendu remains uncertain. Some advocate for its preservation as a unique cultural heritage, while others argue for its adaptation or abandonment.

Alwy M. Jones

The Case of Johan de Witt

Johan de Witt was a prominent Dutch statesman who served as Grand Pensionary of Holland from 1653 to 1672. He was a key figure in the Dutch Golden Age, advocating for a republican form of government and opposing the House of Orange Nassau.

The 1670s were a tumultuous time for the Dutch Republic. The country was facing threats from multiple fronts. Ongoing conflicts with England over maritime supremacy.

In 1672, France invaded the Netherlands, known as the "Rampjaar". Tension between republicans (led by de Witt) and Orangists (supporters of William III of Orange).

On August 20, 1672, Johan de Witt and his brother Cornelis were lynched by an angry mob in The Hague. The brothers were shot, stripped naked, and reportedly had parts of their bodies eaten by the crowd.

De Witt was blamed for the country's military failures against France. The de Witts were seen as too tolerant of Catholics by hardline Calvinists. The war had led to economic hardships, fueling public discontent and William III's supporters painted the de Witts as traitors.

Uruguayan Air Force Flight 571 Crash

On October 13th 1972, Uruguayan Air Force Flight 571, carrying 45 passengers and crew, including members of a rugby team, crashed in the Andes Mountains while en route from Montevideo to Santiago. The plane struck a mountain peak, losing its wings and tail before sliding down a glacier and coming to rest at an altitude of about 11,710 feet.

Of the 45 on board, 12 died in the crash or shortly after. The survivors found themselves in a harsh, frigid environment with limited supplies and no means of communication. They initially believed rescue would come within days.

The survivors used the damaged fuselage as shelter against the extreme cold, they carefully portioned out the limited food supplies from the plane and melted snow for drinking water. Those with medical knowledge tended to the injured as best they could.

Temperatures dropped to -30°C at night and the thin air at high altitude caused health issues. On the 17th day, an avalanche killed eight more survivors. As food supplies dwindled, malnutrition became a severe threat.

After exhausting their food supplies and realizing rescue might not come, the survivors faced a grim choice. They decided to consume the flesh of their dead companions to survive. This decision was reached after much agonizing deliberation and was viewed as a necessary measure to stay alive.

Initial searches were called off after eight days, assuming no survivors. On December 12th, two survivors, Nando Parrado and Roberto Canessa, embarked on a treacherous journey to find help and after a 10 day trek, they encountered a Chilean horseman who alerted authorities. On December 22nd, 72 days after the crash, the remaining 16 survivors were rescued by helicopter.

Alwy M. Jones

The African Origins of C-Sections

The Caesarean section, commonly known as C-section, is a surgical procedure used to deliver a baby through incisions in the abdomen and uterus. While often associated with modern medicine, the roots of this life saving procedure can be traced back to ancient African civilizations.

Contrary to popular belief, the first documented C-sections were not performed in ancient Rome, but in Africa; the Bahima people of Uganda have been performing C-sections since as early as 1800s. Historical evidence suggests that C-sections were performed in Rwanda before they were in Europe. The Zaramo people of Tanzania have a long history of performing abdominal surgeries, including C-sections. These early African C-sections were performed with remarkable success rates, considering the lack of modern medical equipment and antibiotics. Some African cultures viewed C-sections as a way to fulfill spiritual prophecies or overcome curses and the procedure was seen as a way to save mothers when vaginal delivery was impossible. The ability to perform successful C-sections was highly respected in many communities.

Early African C-sections involved sophisticated techniques; banana wine was often used as an anesthetic, specialized knives and other instruments were developed for the procedure. Herbal medicines were used to prevent infection and promote healing.

Alwy M. Jones

The Luo Tribe's Distinctive Rite of Passage

The Luo tribe, one of Kenya's largest ethnic groups primarily residing on the shores and around Lake Victoria, stands out among East African communities for their distinctive coming of age ritual. While all neighboring tribes practice male circumcision as a rite of passage, the Luo have traditionally opted for a different approach: the removal of six lower teeth.

This practice, known as "gino" in the Luo language, has roots tracing back centuries. Historically, it served as a significant marker of adulthood and tribal identity. The exact origins of this custom are not precisely documented, but oral traditions suggest it has been a part of Luo culture for many generations.

Traditionally, when Luo boys reach adolescence, usually between the ages of 12 and 16, they undergo the tooth extraction process. The six lower front teeth, specifically the incisors and canines, are removed using specialized tools. In the past, this was done by skilled elders, though in more recent times, some have sought the assistance of dental professionals.

The gap created by the missing teeth serves as a visible marker of Luo identity, distinguishing them from other ethnic groups. Like circumcision in other tribes, tooth extraction symbolizes the transition from childhood to adulthood. Many Luo view this practice as a source of cultural pride and a link to their ancestors.

Some anthropologists suggest that historically, the practice may have had practical purposes, such as facilitating feeding during lockjaw, a condition that was once more common in the region. The Luo is the only tribe in Kenya that traditionally did not practice male circumcision, making the tooth extraction ritual particularly significant.

In recent decades, the practice of tooth extraction has become less common among the Luo.

Alwy M. Jones

The Cult of Cybele

Cybele, the Phrygian mother goddess, held a significant place in ancient Mediterranean religions. Her worship, originating in Anatolia (modern day Turkey), spread throughout the Greek and Roman worlds, bringing with it unique and sometimes controversial practices.

Cybele's cult dates back to at least the 7th century BCE in Phrygia. As her worship spread, she became associated with Greek and Roman deities, often identified with Rhea or Ops. In 204 BCE, amid the Second Punic War, Rome officially adopted her cult, marking a significant cultural and religious shift.

Cybele was revered as the mother of gods, embodying nature's fertile and wild aspects. Her myths often involved her youthful consort Attis, whose death and resurrection symbolized the cycle of seasons and nature's rebirth.

Known as metroons, Cybele's temples were centers of worship and ritual. The most important was the spring festival of Megalensia, celebrating Attis' resurrection. These often involved ecstatic music, dancing, self-flagellation and Taurobolium; a later practice involving ritual bathing in bull's blood.

Central to Cybele's cult were the Galli, her priesthood of castrated males. In a frenzied state, initiates would castrate themselves, mirroring the myth of Attis. Galli wore women's clothing and elaborate jewelry (crossdressing).

They engaged in wild dances to the rhythm of drums and cymbals. Galli often traveled, seeking alms and offering prophecies.

It represented one of the first "eastern" religions adopted by Rome, paving the way for others. The Galli challenged traditional notions of gender roles and sexuality. The cult's emotional, personal approach to worship influenced later religious movements. Roman elites sometimes used the cult for political purposes, demonstrating Rome's inclusivity. The cult's practices, especially those of the Galli, often faced criticism and ridicule from conservative Romans.

Modern scholars view the cult of Cybele as a complex phenomenon that reveals much about ancient attitudes towards gender, sexuality, and religious ecstasy. The voluntary castration of the Galli has been interpreted variously as an extreme form of devotion, a way of transcending human limitations, or a reflection of ancient concepts of gender fluidity. Some researchers also note parallels between Cybele's cult and other ancient mystery religions, suggesting a broader pattern of personal, emotionally intense religious experiences in the ancient world.

Alwy M. Jones

The Roman Festival That Shaped Modern Celebrations

Saturnalia, one of ancient Rome's most popular festivals, was a time of revelry, role reversal, and religious observance that has left an indelible mark on Western cultural traditions. This weeklong celebration, held in honor of the god Saturn, offers fascinating insights into Roman society and continues to influence modern holiday customs.

Saturnalia was celebrated from December 17th-23rd in the Julian calendar. Its origins are believed to date back to archaic Roman times, possibly as early as the 5th century BCE. The festival honored Saturn, the god of agriculture, abundance, and time.

Perhaps the most striking aspect of Saturnalia was the temporary inversion of social roles. Slaves were allowed to criticize their masters, wear their clothes, and be waited upon at meals. This custom reflected the myth of Saturn's rule as a time of social equality. The exchange of small gifts (sigillaria) was a central part of the festivities, often including wax candles and small clay figurines.

Elaborate meals and continuous parties were common throughout the celebration. Normally frowned upon, gambling was permitted and even encouraged during Saturnalia. In many households, a "King of Saturnalia" was chosen to preside over the merrymaking, often issuing ridiculous commands to other family members. The festival began with a sacrifice at the Temple of Saturn, followed by a public banquet and shouting of the phrase "Io Saturnalia!" in the streets.

Alwy M. Jones

The Archimimus

In the complex tapestry of ancient Roman society, few figures were as paradoxical and fascinating as the Archimimus, or Funeral Clown. This unique profession exemplified the Roman penchant for blending the sacred and the profane, challenging our modern notions of appropriate funerary behavior. The role of the Archimimus emerged during the late Republican and early Imperial periods of Rome, roughly from the 1st century BCE to the 2nd century CE. This era was marked by elaborate funerary customs, particularly for the elite, reflecting the Romans' complex relationship with death and the afterlife. The primary function of the Archimimus was to impersonate the deceased during the funeral procession. Wearing a mask molded in the likeness of the dead and dressed in their clothes, the Archimimus would mimic the mannerisms, voice, and even notable sayings of the departed. Despite the somber occasion, the Archimimus was expected to provide moments of levity. They would often engage in exaggerated imitations of the deceased's quirks or recount humorous anecdotes from their life. The Archimimus had a unique license to speak freely about the deceased, sometimes even mocking their flaws or questionable deeds. This served as a form of social catharsis and, arguably, a final judgment on the person's character. The presence of the Archimimus was believed to aid in the transition of the deceased to the afterlife, serving as a bridge between the world of the living and the dead.

Alwy M. Jones

A Culture Written on the Body

The Surma people, also known as the Suri, are an ethnic group residing in the southwestern part of Ethiopia, near the border with South Sudan. Their distinctive body modification practices, particularly lip discs and scarification, have fascinated anthropologists and travelers alike for generations.

The Surma have inhabited their current territory for centuries, maintaining a semi-nomadic, pastoral lifestyle. Their isolation has allowed them to preserve many traditional practices, including their striking body modifications, which are deeply intertwined with their cultural identity.

One of the most recognizable features of Surma culture is the practice of wearing large lip discs, primarily by women.

The lower lip is pierced, usually around the age of 15-18, then the hole is gradually stretched over months or years. Increasingly larger discs, traditionally made of clay or wood, are inserted.

The lip disc is a proud marker of Surma identity and the larger discs are traditionally considered more beautiful. The size of the disc can influence the bride price in marriages. The process marks the transition to womanhood.

- Surma Woman with lower lip plug

Alwy M. Jones

The Bodi Tribe's Celebration of Male Corpulence

In the Omo Valley of southwestern Ethiopia, the Bodi tribe, also known as Me'en, practice a remarkable tradition that challenges Western beauty standards. Here, men with larger bellies are considered the most attractive and desirable, leading to a unique cultural practice centered around deliberate weight gain.

The Bodi are primarily pastoralists, with cattle playing a central role in their society. Their isolated location has allowed them to maintain many traditional practices, including their distinctive beauty standards. At the heart of the Bodi's appreciation for male corpulence is the Ka'el ceremony, an annual competition to crown the fattest man.

For six months, unmarried men consume a diet of blood and milk to gain weight. They live in isolation, minimizing physical activity to maximize weight gain. At the ceremony, they parade their enlarged bellies before the tribe and a winner is chosen based on who has achieved the most impressive girth.

A large belly indicates wealth and the ability to afford excess food. In a region prone to food scarcity, extra weight suggests good health. Larger men are often seen as better suited for leadership roles. Bodi women typically find larger men more desirable as partners.

Alwy M. Jones

Researchers studying the Bodi note that their beauty standards, while striking to outsiders, are deeply logical within their cultural context. The practice demonstrates how beauty ideals are culturally constructed and can vary dramatically between societies.

Some anthropologists argue that the Bodi's appreciation for larger male bodies serves as a form of "conspicuous consumption," displaying wealth and status through physical form.

Alwy M. Jones

The Tragic Story of George Stinney Jr.

In the annals of American justice, few cases are as heartbreaking and disturbing as that of George Stinney Jr., a 14 year old African American boy who became the youngest person executed in the United States in the 20th century. His story is a stark reminder of the racial injustices that have plagued the American legal system and the devastating consequences of rushed judgments in capital cases.

On March 23rd 1944, in the small mill town of Alcolu, South Carolina, two young white girls, Betty June Binnicker, 11, and Mary Emma Thames, 8, were found brutally murdered. George Stinney Jr., who had been seen talking to the girls earlier that day, quickly became the prime suspect. Within hours of the discovery, Stinney was arrested and interrogated by police, alone, without his parents or an attorney present. What transpired in that room would seal his fate.

The trial of George Stinney Jr. was a travesty of justice from start to finish. The entire trial lasted just one day. An all-white jury was selected. Stinney's court appointed lawyer, a tax commissioner with political ambitions, offered no defense, called no witnesses, and failed to file an appeal. The primary evidence was a confession that Stinney allegedly made during interrogation, though no written record of this confession exists. After only 10 minutes of deliberation, the jury found Stinney guilty. On June 16th 1944, less than three months after the murders,

George Stinney Jr. was executed by electric chair. At 5'1" and just 95 pounds, he was so small that the straps of the chair didn't fit him properly, and an electrode was too big for his leg. His Bible, which he carried with him, was used as a booster seat.

Witnesses reported that Stinney cried throughout the execution process. It took several jolts of electricity before he was pronounced dead.

For 70 years, the Stinney family and civil rights advocates fought to have the case reexamined. Their efforts finally bore fruit in 2014. Affidavits from Stinney's siblings provided alibis for his whereabouts on the day of the murder. Experts testified that the confession was likely coerced and implausible given the physical evidence. Circuit Court Judge Carmen Mullen reviewed the case and vacated Stinney's conviction, stating that he had not received a fair trial.

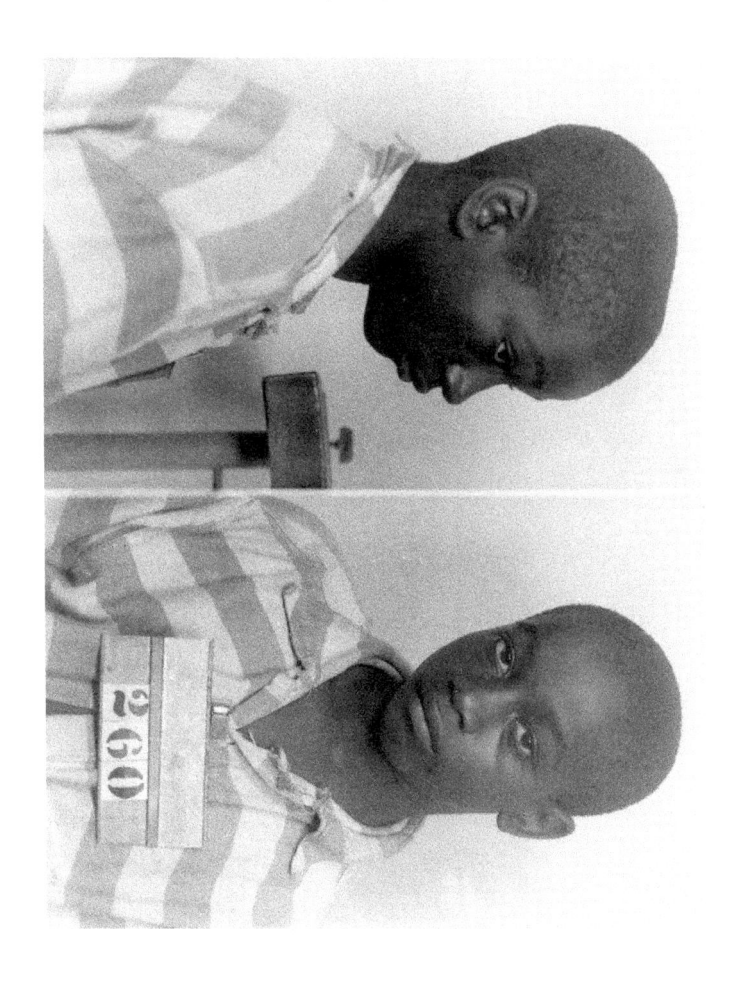

- 14 Year old George Stinney Jr. mugshot

- George Stinney (second from right) being led to the execution chamber.

Alwy M. Jones

The Ancient Roman Art of Haruspicy

In the complex tapestry of ancient Roman religion, few practices were as simultaneously revered and controversial as haruspicy; the art of divining the will of the gods through the examination of animal entrails. This unique form of divination played a crucial role in Roman decision-making, particularly during times of crisis, and offers fascinating insights into the intersection of politics, religion, and society in ancient Rome.

Haruspicy, while deeply ingrained in Roman religious practice, actually originated with the Etruscans, a civilization that preceded and greatly influenced Roman culture. The Romans adopted this practice around the 3rd century BCE, and it quickly became an integral part of their state religion.

The Haruspices were specially trained religious officials, often of Etruscan descent, who performed the divination. An animal, typically a sheep, ox, or chicken, was sacrificed. The haruspex would examine various organs, particularly the liver, which was considered the seat of life. Special attention was paid to the size, shape, color, and any abnormalities in the organs. The findings were interpreted as messages from the gods, providing guidance on important matters of state and predicting future events.

The liver held particular importance in haruspicy. So crucial was this organ that bronze models of sheep livers, divided into sections corresponding to different divine and cosmic influences, were used for training and reference. One famous example, the Liver of Piacenza, survives to this day.

Magistrates and generals often consulted haruspices before making important decisions, effectively giving religious sanction to political actions. During times of crisis, such as plagues, wars, or natural disasters, haruspicy was used to determine the cause of divine displeasure and the appropriate remedies. Emperors used favorable haruspicial readings to legitimize their rule and decisions. The practice served as a means of social control, with the haruspices' interpretations often aligning with the interests of the ruling class.

Some Romans, including prominent figures like Cicero, expressed skepticism about the practice, suggesting it was open to manipulation for political ends. There was ongoing tension about the Etruscan origins of the practice, with some seeing it as un-Roman. As Greek philosophical ideas spread in Rome, some intellectuals questioned the rational basis of haruspicy.

Alwy M. Jones

The Dark Ages for Felines

In the annals of human history, few practices are as unsettling as the medieval custom of burning cats. This disturbing phenomenon, which reached its peak in 13th century Europe, reflects the complex interplay of superstition, religious fervor, and misguided attempts at pest control that characterized the Middle Ages.

The practice of cat burning emerged during a tumultuous period in European history, marked by plagues, wars, and significant social upheaval. Cats, once revered in ancient cultures like Egypt, found themselves at the center of a perfect storm of negative associations.

In 1233, Pope Gregory IX issued the papal bull "Vox in Rama," which associated cats, particularly black cats, with heresy and Satan worship. This proclamation gave religious sanction to the persecution of cats, leading to widespread killings. Cats were often associated with witches and dark magic in medieval folklore. The belief that witches could transform into cats fueled fears and persecution.

Ironically, as cat populations decreased, rat populations surged, contributing to the spread of diseases like the bubonic plague.

Cat burning took various forms but was often incorporated into public festivities and rituals. In France and Belgium, cats were sometimes thrown into bonfires as part of Midsummer celebrations. In 1730s Paris, apprentice printers conducted a mock trial of cats before hanging and burning them. In some areas, cats were paraded through towns in wicker baskets before being burned alive.

The persecution of cats often had underlying political and religious motivations. Cats became symbolic scapegoats in the fight against heretical movements like the Cathars. Public cat burnings served as a form of social spectacle and control, reinforcing religious and political authority. The association of cats with witchcraft disproportionately affected women, who were more often accused of witchcraft.

The Startling History of Trepanning

Trepanning, also known as trephination or craniotomy, is one of the oldest known surgical procedures in human history. This practice, which involves drilling or scraping a hole into the human skull, has been performed for thousands of years and across various cultures. Its persistence throughout history, despite its seemingly barbaric nature, offers fascinating insights into the evolution of medical understanding and the human drive to heal.

Archaeological evidence suggests that trepanning dates back to the Neolithic period, around 7,000 years ago. Trepanned skulls have been found across the globe, from Europe and Africa to South America, indicating that this was a widespread practice.

Medieval and ancient doctors had various theories about why trepanning could be beneficial. Many ancient cultures believed that evil spirits causing mental illnesses or headaches could be released through the hole. It was also thought that trepanning could relieve pressure on the brain caused by trauma or other conditions. Epilepsy and other seizure disorders were sometimes treated with trepanning. Chronic head pain was another common reason for performing the procedure. Various forms of mental illness were believed to be treatable through trepanning. In some cases, trepanning was used as a method of bloodletting, believed to balance the body's "humors."

Surprisingly, many individuals survived the procedure. Archaeological Evidence from many skulls show signs of healing, indicating that the patient survived the operation and lived for years afterward. The biggest danger was likely infection, particularly in pre-antibiotic eras. In some cases, such as treating subdural hematomas (blood clots on the brain), trepanning may have actually been beneficial. Placebo Effect; the psychological impact of the procedure may have led to perceived improvements in some patients.

Notable Historical Figures:

1. Hippocrates: The ancient Greek physician wrote about trepanning for head injuries in his work "On Injuries of the Head."

2. Galen: This influential Roman physician also discussed trepanning, influencing medieval medical practices.

3. Ambroise Pare: A 16th century French surgeon who improved trepanning techniques and tools.

Alwy M. Jones

Till Death Do Us Part

In an era when divorce was generally frowned upon and difficult to obtain, some medieval communities in Europe had a startlingly unconventional method for ending a marriage; trial by combat. This practice, as absurd as it may seem to modern sensibilities, was a real, albeit rare, occurrence in certain regions, particularly in parts of Germany and Scandinavia.

The man would be placed in a circular pit dug in the ground, about waist deep with one of his hands tied behind his back.

The woman would be free to move around the edge of the pit. She was armed with a unique weapon with three rocks wrapped tightly in cloth, tied together to form a makeshift flail.

The husband was given a short stick or club to defend himself.

The combat had specific rules and potential outcomes. If the husband managed to strike his wife with his club, he won the contest. If the wife struck her husband on the head with her cloth-wrapped rocks three times, she was declared the victor.

The winner of the combat would be granted the divorce. The loser faced consequences beyond just losing the marriage; they could be fined or even executed in some cases.

Alwy M. Jones

The Bizarre World of Medieval Animal Trials

In the annals of legal history, few practices are as perplexing to modern sensibilities as the medieval custom of putting animals on trial. From the 13th to the 17th century, numerous European countries, including France, Italy, and Switzerland, held formal legal proceedings against animals accused of various crimes. These trials, while seemingly absurd today, reveal much about medieval society's understanding of justice, morality, and the natural world.

Animal trials were conducted with all the pomp and circumstance of human trials; animals were assigned lawyers, witnesses were called, and evidence was presented. Accusations ranged from murder to crop destruction. If found guilty, animals could face execution, exile, or even excommunication.

Several factors contributed to this unusual legal practice; medieval people often attributed human like reasoning to animals with claims that Old Testament passages suggested animals could be held accountable for their actions. These trials provided a sense of control over unpredictable natural events, some believed that punishing animals would deter similar actions in the future.

Pigs, dogs, and cattle were common defendants and wild animals, like insects and rodents were sometimes put on trial. In rare cases, trials were held for werewolves and other legendary beasts.

Case Studies:

1. The Sow of Falaise (1386):

   A sow in Falaise, Normandy, was tried for killing and partially eating an infant. The pig was found guilty, dressed in human clothes, and publicly executed by hanging.

2. The Rats of Autun (1522):

   In one of the most famous cases, rats were put on trial for destroying barley crops. The rats' appointed lawyer, Bartholomew Chassenee, successfully argued for their acquittal, claiming his clients hadn't received proper summons to court.

3. The Caterpillars of Vaud (1451):

   A group of caterpillars were tried for damaging crops in the Swiss canton of Vaud. They were ordered to be excommunicated from the church.

4. The Dog of Savigny-sur-Etang (1457):

   A dog was sentenced to death by hanging for killing a child. The dog was dressed in human clothes and hanged from a gallows in the town square.

Alwy M. Jones

Shaping Beauty and Power

In the lush forests of what is now the Democratic Republic of Congo, the Mangbetu people practiced a striking custom that quite literally shaped their society. Known as Lipombo, the practice of artificial cranial deformation was a defining feature of Mangbetu culture, particularly among the ruling classes.

Lipombo involved the deliberate elongation of the skull, typically beginning in infancy. From birth, an infant's head would be tightly wrapped with cloth bandages, as the child grew, the bandages would be progressively tightened. This process continued until the desired elongation was achieved, usually in early childhood. The forehead and back of the skull would grow upward and backward, creating a distinctly elongated shape.

For the Mangbetu, Lipombo was far more than an aesthetic choice. It held deep cultural significance; the practice was primarily associated with the ruling classes and elite members of society. It visually distinguished the nobility from commoners. Elongated heads were considered highly attractive in Mangbetu culture, it influenced standards of beauty for both men and women. The Mangbetu believed that the practice increased cranial capacity which was associated with higher intelligence and wisdom. The distinctive silhouette created by Lipombo was seen as regal and commanding. It reinforced the authority of rulers and nobles. Lipombo became a defining feature of Mangbetu identity, it distinguished them from neighboring tribes and cultures.

The practice of cranial deformation was not unique to the Mangbetu. Similar customs have been observed in various cultures worldwide, from ancient Egyptians to certain Native American tribes. However, the Mangbetu's practice stood out for its pronounced effect and its persistence into the early 20th century.

- Postcard showing Mangbetu woman with skull deformity.

Medieval Medicine's Burning Question

In the often brutal world of medieval medicine, few treatments were as cringe inducing as those used for hemorrhoids. Medieval physicians, drawing on ancient Greek and Roman medical texts, believed hemorrhoids were caused by an excess of black bile in the body. They were seen as both a symptom of humoral imbalance and a way for the body to purge itself of harmful substances.

The primary treatment for severe hemorrhoids was cauterization using hot irons; the cautery iron would be heated until red-hot. The physician would then apply the iron directly to the hemorrhoid, this process was believed to both remove the hemorrhoid and seal the wound.

Cauterization was thought to "dry up" the excess humors causing the hemorrhoids, the intense heat was believed to restore balance to the affected area.

For less severe cases, physicians might attempt to remove hemorrhoids manually; the doctor would use their fingernails to scrape or tear off the hemorrhoid. This was often done without anesthesia, relying only on the patient's tolerance for pain.

Manual removal was seen as a way to physically extract the "bad" humors from the body. Some physicians believed that the pain involved in the procedure was therapeutic in itself.

Alwy M. Jones

The Royal Flush

In the intricate hierarchy of medieval and Tudor royal courts, few positions were as paradoxically prestigious and intimate as that of the Groom of the Stool. This role, which existed from the 11th to the 17th century, particularly in the English royal household, was simultaneously one of the highest honors and most unpalatable duties a courtier could aspire to.

The position of Groom of the Stool originated from the Old English word "stool," which referred to a close stool or portable commode. Over time, the role evolved from a simple domestic servant to a position of significant political influence.

The Groom of the Stool's primary duty was to assist the monarch in their most private moments, specifically during defecation. This included helping the monarch use the close stool, cleaning them afterward, and disposing of the waste.

The Groom was responsible for the king's clothing, especially his undergarments. They would ensure the monarch was properly dressed and that their clothes were clean and in good repair. Helping the monarch bathe and maintaining their personal hygiene was another key responsibility. The Groom often slept in the same room as the king to be available at all times. Due to their intimate access, the Groom often became a trusted confidant and advisor to the monarch.

Despite its seemingly undignified nature, the position held immense political power. The Groom had unparalleled private access to the king, more than any other courtier or even family members, this access allowed for significant influence over royal decisions and policies.

The Groom could control who had access to the king, making them a crucial intermediary for those seeking royal favor. In later years, the role expanded to include management of the Privy Purse, the monarch's personal funds, this financial control further enhanced the position's power and prestige.

The Groom could use their influence to secure positions and favors for friends and allies.

Notable Grooms of the Stool:

Several Grooms of the Stool went on to have significant political careers:

1. Hugh Denys (served Henry VII)

2. Sir Anthony Denny (served Henry VIII)

3. Sir John Pakington (served Elizabeth I)

- William III's close stool

Crushed by Justice

In the annals of medieval justice, few punishments were as gruesome and torturous as execution by pressing, also known as "peine forte et dure" (strong and hard punishment). This brutal method of execution, which involved slowly crushing an accused criminal to death, serves as a stark reminder of the harsh realities of medieval justice systems.

Execution by pressing emerged in England during the 13th century and persisted until the 18th century. It was not technically a form of execution, but rather a coercive measure used to force accused individuals to enter a plea in court.

When an accused person refused to enter a plea of guilty or not guilty, they would be subjected to pressing. The accused would be laid on their back on the ground, a wooden board would be placed on their chest. Heavy weights, often stones, would be piled onto the board. More weight would be added each day until the accused either entered a plea or died. The accused would be given only moldy bread and dirty water on alternating days.

Several factors contributed to the use of this brutal practice. If an accused died without entering a plea, they would die unconvicted, allowing their property to pass to their heirs rather than being forfeited to the crown. The brutality of the punishment was meant to deter others from refusing to plead. Some viewed the suffering as a form of penance for the accused's crimes.

Notable Cases:

1. Giles Corey (1692):

Perhaps the most famous victim of pressing, Corey was accused of witchcraft during the Salem witch trials. He refused to enter a plea and was pressed to death over three days, allegedly uttering "More weight" as his final words.

2. Margaret Clitherow (1586):

Executed for harboring Catholic priests in Protestant England. She refused to enter a plea to protect her children from being forced to testify against her.

The Case of Nong Youhui:

Nong Youhui is a boy from Dahua, China, who gained attention in 2009 when he was reported to have unusually bright blue green eyes and the ability to see clearly in the dark. He was nicknamed "Cat Boy" due to these alleged feline like traits.

Some speculate that Nong might have developed a structure similar to the tapetum lucidum found in cats and other nocturnal animals. This reflective layer behind the retina enhances night vision by reflecting light back through the retina.

Another theory suggests a rare genetic mutation affecting the structures of Nong's eyes, possibly related to the genes responsible for eye color and light sensitivity.

Some hypothesize that Nong might have an unusually high number of rod cells, which are responsible for night vision in humans.

If confirmed, this case could lead to breakthroughs in understanding human vision and potential treatments for night blindness. It might provide insights into human adaptation and the potential for developing enhanced sensory abilities.

Similar Cases:

1. "Human owl" case: In 2014, a woman in the UK claimed to have superior night vision, though her case was not as widely reported or verified as Nong's.

2. Tetrachromacy: While not related to night vision, some individuals have been documented to have a fourth type of cone cell in their eyes, allowing them to see a wider range of colors than the average person.

Alwy M. Jones

The Forgotten Voyage

In the annals of history, some stories remain hidden, overshadowed by more widely accepted narratives. One such tale is that of Abubakari II, the mariner prince of Mali, who is said to have embarked on an extraordinary voyage across the Atlantic Ocean in 1311, long before Christopher Columbus set sail.

Abubakari II, also known as Mansa Abu Bakr II, was the ruler of the Mali Empire, one of the wealthiest and most powerful states in 14th century Africa. Driven by curiosity and a desire to explore the limits of the ocean, Abubakari reportedly abdicated his throne to pursue this ambitious maritime expedition.

According to oral traditions and some historical accounts, Abubakari II assembled a fleet of 200 ships and set sail westward into the Atlantic. His motivations were multifaceted; to satisfy his exploratory spirit, to expand trade routes, and to spread the influence of Mali beyond the African continent.

After a journey of several weeks, Abubakari's fleet is said to have reached the shores of what we now know as the Americas. Unlike later European explorers, Abubakari reportedly approached this new land with respect and curiosity, acknowledging that it was already inhabited by indigenous peoples.

The prince turned explorer established peaceful contact with the native populations, engaging in trade and cultural exchange. This interaction would have been groundbreaking, representing one of the earliest known transatlantic contacts between Africa and the Americas.

Abubakari's acknowledgment of the existing civilizations in the Americas stands in stark contrast to later European attitudes. He recognized the sovereignty and cultural richness of the indigenous peoples, viewing them as potential trading partners rather than subjects to be conquered.

The significance of this voyage, if verified, would be immense. It would challenge the Eurocentric view of world history, demonstrating that African mariners had the capability and courage to cross the Atlantic long before European explorers. It would also provide evidence of early peaceful interactions between African and American civilizations.

However, it's important to note that while this story is compelling, it remains controversial among historians. The lack of contemporary written records and archaeological evidence has led many scholars to question the veracity of the account. The story of Abubakari II's voyage has been primarily preserved through oral traditions, which can be difficult to verify.

Alwy M. Jones

The Forging of a Soviet Icon

In the annals of 20th century history, few figures loom as large as Joseph Stalin. Yet, before he became the iron-fisted ruler of the Soviet Union, he was known by a different name: Joseph Vissarionovich Djugashvili.

Born in 1878 in Gori, Georgia, then part of the Russian Empire, Joseph Djugashvili grew up in a region with a complex cultural and political identity. Georgia, with its distinct language and traditions, had a long history of resistance against foreign rule. This context is crucial in understanding the future dictator's early life and his eventual transformation into "Stalin."

The name Djugashvili, while common in Georgia, was difficult for many Russians to pronounce and remember. As a rising figure in the Bolshevik movement, Joseph recognized the need for a more impactful, Russian friendly name. His choice of "Stalin," meaning "Man of Steel" in Russian, was a calculated decision that reflected both his personal ambitions and the political climate of the time.

The adoption of "Stalin" as a revolutionary pseudonym occurred around 1912, during a period of intense political activity and growing tensions within the Russian Empire. This name change can be seen as a strategic move in several ways; by choosing a Russian name, Stalin distanced himself from his Georgian roots, presenting himself as a figure of pan-

Soviet appeal. This was crucial in a movement that emphasized international worker solidarity over national identities.

"Man of Steel" evoked images of industrial might, resilience, and unwavering resolve, qualities that resonated with the Bolshevik ideals of the time. It also aligned with the Soviet emphasis on rapid industrialization and the cult of the worker.

Unlike his Georgian name, "Stalin" was easy for Russians to pronounce and remember, aiding in his rise to prominence within the party. The name change was part of a broader effort to craft a public image. Stalin was presenting himself not just as a political leader, but as an embodiment of Soviet ideals.

The transformation from Djugashvili to Stalin also reflected the complex relationship between Georgia and Russia. While Stalin downplayed his Georgian heritage in his public persona, he never completely abandoned it. This duality; a Georgian leading a Russian dominated state would have significant implications for Soviet nationality policies.

Stalin's name change can be seen as a microcosm of the broader Soviet project of creating a new society and a new type of person. Just as he remade himself from a Georgian seminary student into the "Man of Steel," Stalin would later attempt to remake the entire Soviet Union in his image.

The impact of this name change extended far beyond Stalin's personal life. As he rose to power, "Stalin" became synonymous with the Soviet state itself. The cult of personality that developed around him was intrinsically linked to the imagery evoked by his chosen name; strength, permanence, and unyielding will.

However, it's important to note that while Stalin presented himself as the embodiment of Soviet ideals, his rule was marked by brutal repression, including against his native Georgia. The name that once symbolized strength and progress became associated with terror and totalitarianism.

Alwy M. Jones

The Posthumous Indignity of Saartjie Baartman

In the annals of scientific history, few cases are as ethically fraught and culturally sensitive as that of Saartjie Baartman, also known as Sarah or Sara Baartman. Born in the late 18th century in what is now South Africa, Baartman's life and death became a stark illustration of racial exploitation, scientific racism, and the dehumanization of indigenous peoples. Baartman, a Khoikhoi woman, was brought to Europe in 1810 and exhibited as a freak show attraction due to her physical features, particularly her buttocks and genitalia. Her exploitation continued even after her death in 1815, when French anatomist Georges Cuvier acquired her body.

Cuvier, a prominent zoologist and paleontologist of his time, dissected Baartman's body in the name of scientific inquiry. However, his actions reflect the deeply problematic attitudes of 19th century European science towards non-European peoples. Cuvier's treatment of Baartman's remains was not just a violation of human dignity but also a manifestation of the racist pseudoscience that sought to categorize and hierarchize human races. There's no evidence that Baartman consented to the posthumous use of her body for scientific study or display. By treating Baartman's body as a specimen rather than human remains deserving of respect, Cuvier perpetuated the dehumanization Baartman experienced in life.

The focus on Baartman's physical features, particularly her genitalia, reflects the objectification and sexualization of African women's bodies by Europeans. Cuvier's work contributed to the development of racist theories that attempted to justify European colonialism and the subjugation of non-European peoples. Perhaps most disturbingly, parts of Baartman's body, including her preserved brain and genitals, were displayed at the Musee de l'Homme (Museum of Man) in Paris until 1974. This prolonged exhibition, lasting well into the 20th century, raises serious questions about the slow progress of ethical standards in scientific and museum practices. The exhibition extended Baartman's exploitation long after her death, denying her dignity even in death. The focus on her physical features perpetuated harmful stereotypes about African bodies. The long duration of the display suggests a failure of museum officials to reckon with the ethical implications of exhibiting human remains, especially those obtained under dubious circumstances. The exhibition showed a lack of respect for Khoikhoi cultural practices and beliefs regarding death and burial. It wasn't until 2002, following years of campaigning by the post-apartheid South African government, that Baartman's remains were finally returned to her homeland for a proper burial. This delay in repatriation highlights the ongoing struggles many indigenous communities face in reclaiming ancestral remains from museums and scientific institutions worldwide.

- Caricature of Baartman by William Heath (1810)

Alwy M. Jones

The Agricultural Innovator Who Revolutionized the South

George Washington Carver, born into slavery in the early 1860s in Diamond, Missouri, rose to become one of the most influential agricultural scientists of the 20th century. His work not only transformed Southern agriculture but also significantly improved the economic prospects of many African American farmers.

Despite facing numerous obstacles due to racial discrimination, Carver pursued education with remarkable determination. He became the first African American to earn a Bachelor of Science degree from Iowa State Agricultural College (now Iowa State University) in 1894. He later earned his Master of Science degree in bacterial botany and agriculture in 1896.

In 1896, Booker T. Washington invited Carver to head the Agriculture Department at Tuskegee Institute in Alabama. This position became the platform from which Carver would launch his most impactful work.

Carver's research focused on finding alternative crops to cotton and developing new products from these crops. His work was crucial in addressing two significant issues; years of cotton monoculture had severely depleted Southern soils. Carver promoted crop rotation, introducing nitrogen-fixing plants like peanuts, soybeans, and sweet potatoes to restore soil fertility. By developing numerous products from these crops, Carver created new markets for farmers, reducing their reliance on cotton.

Carver is perhaps best known for his work with peanuts, developed over 300 products from peanuts, including:

- Foods: Milk, cheese, flour, vinegar, and cooking oils

- Industrial products: Soap, cosmetics, dyes, and plastics

- Medicinal applications: Antiseptics and goiter treatments

This research not only provided farmers with alternative crops but also stimulated industrial demand for these products.

Carver's work extended beyond peanuts. He developed about 118 products from sweet potatoes, including flour, vinegar, starch, synthetic rubber, and postage stamp glue. From soybeans, he created about 100 products, including plastics and a synthetic marble.

Carver's interest in mycology (the study of fungi) led to significant contributions in plant pathology. He identified and developed treatments for various fungal diseases affecting crops, further improving agricultural yields.

Carver was not content with laboratory research alone. He actively worked to disseminate his findings to farmers; he developed "movable schools" to bring agricultural education directly to farmers. Carver published 44 practical bulletins for farmers, providing accessible information on crops and cultivation techniques. He also traveled extensively, giving lectures on agriculture and nutrition.

George Washington Carver's work went far beyond simple agricultural innovation. By providing alternatives to cotton and developing new products from these crops, he helped diversify the Southern economy and improve the economic status of many African American farmers. His emphasis on sustainability and natural methods in agriculture was far ahead of his time.

Carver's legacy extends beyond his scientific achievements. As an African American scientist achieving prominence in the early 20th century, he became a role model for many, demonstrating the potential for African Americans to excel in scientific fields despite pervasive racial barriers.

George Washington Carver died on January 5, 1943, but his impact on agriculture, botany, and chemistry continues to be felt today. His life's work stands as a testament to the power of scientific innovation to drive economic and social change, and his methods of sustainable agriculture remain relevant in our ongoing quest for environmental stewardship.

Alwy M. Jones

Exploring the Dani Tribe's Unique Mourning Ritual

In the lush highlands of Papua, Indonesia, the Dani tribe practices a mourning ritual that may seem shocking to outsiders but holds deep cultural significance for their community.

When a close family member dies, Dani women traditionally have the upper portion of one of their fingers cut off. This practice, known as Iki Palek, is typically performed using a stone axe. The amputated finger joint is then dried and burned, with the ashes being stored in a special place.

The Dani tribe, numbering around 250,000 people, has inhabited the Baliem Valley of Papua for thousands of years. Their isolated location has allowed them to maintain many traditional practices, including this unique mourning ritual, despite increasing contact with the outside world in recent decades.

The amputation serves as a visible, permanent reminder of the loss. The physical pain is believed to be a reflection of the emotional pain of losing a loved one. The Dani believe that the pain and blood sacrifice help to drive away evil spirits and satisfy the ghosts of the dead. The shared experience of this ritual reinforces tribal bonds and provides a communal outlet for grief. The willingness to endure this painful ritual is seen as a demonstration of love and respect for the deceased.

It's notable that this practice is exclusively performed by women. This reflects the Dani's gender roles, where women are often seen as the primary bearers of emotional burdens within the family and community.

The loss of finger joints can have practical implications for the women's daily activities, particularly in a society where manual labor is crucial for survival. However, the Dani view these difficulties as a continued reminder of their lost loved ones and a testament to their emotional strength.

Alwy M. Jones

Desperation, Duty, and a Royal Heir

In the annals of European royal history, few stories are as tragic and disturbing as that of Maria Eleonora of Brandenburg and her relationship with her daughter, Christina of Sweden. This tale sheds light on the immense pressures faced by royal women in the 17th century and the devastating consequences of the obsession with male heirs.

Maria Eleonora of Brandenburg was born in 1599 to John Sigismund, Elector of Brandenburg, and Anna of Prussia. In 1620, she married King Gustavus Adolphus of Sweden, entering into a union that would be marked by personal turmoil and political strife.

Like many royal women of her time, Maria Eleonora faced immense pressure to produce a male heir. This pressure was particularly acute in Sweden, where the king was deeply involved in the Thirty Years' War and needed a clear line of succession to ensure stability.

On December 8th 1626, Maria Eleonora gave birth to a child. Initially believed to be a boy due to the child's reported hairiness and strong cry, it was soon discovered that the infant was, in fact, a girl. This revelation was met with great disappointment, particularly by Maria Eleonora herself.

According to historical accounts, Maria Eleonora's disappointment and mental instability led her to attempt to harm her infant daughter multiple times. She allegedly tried to throw the baby out of a window, only to be stopped by courtiers. There were also reports of her attempting to drop the child "by accident." And in some sources suggest she even tried to starve the infant.

Alwy M. Jones

A Royal Delusion Examined

In the annals of royal eccentricities, few stories are as intriguing as that of Princess Alexandra of Bavaria and her firm belief that she had swallowed a glass grand piano. This peculiar tale from the 19th century offers a fascinating glimpse into the intersection of royal life, mental health, and the medical understanding of the time.

Princess Alexandra Amalie of Bavaria was born on October 26th 1826, to King Ludwig I of Bavaria and Therese of Saxe-Hildburghausen. She lived during a time of significant change in Europe, with the Industrial Revolution in full swing and scientific understanding rapidly advancing.

According to historical accounts, Princess Alexandra, in her early twenties, became convinced that she had swallowed a glass grand piano as a child. This belief persisted despite its obvious physical impossibility. She was reportedly so concerned about the imaginary instrument inside her that she would walk sideways through doorways, fearing that moving straight ahead would cause the piano to shatter.

From a modern perspective, Princess Alexandra's belief bears hallmarks of what we now recognize as delusional disorder. The princess held onto this idea despite clear evidence to the contrary. While unusual, the concept of swallowing an object is more plausible than some other types of delusions. Despite this belief, Alexandra was able to carry out her royal duties to some extent.

While no definitive medical explanation was provided at the time, several theories have been proposed by modern researchers. Some suggest that Alexandra might have suffered from a digestive disorder, with the piano delusion being a misinterpretation of her physical discomfort. The fear of breaking the "glass piano" could be seen as a manifestation of broader anxieties. The specific nature of her fear and her behavioral adaptations (walking sideways) align with some OCD symptoms. While less likely due to the isolated nature of her delusion, it cannot be entirely ruled out.

Alwy M. Jones

Charles VI of France and His Fragile Reign

In the annals of French history, few monarchs have left as complex a legacy as Charles VI, also known as Charles the Mad or the Beloved. His 42 year reign (1380-1422) was marked by periods of lucidity interspersed with bouts of severe mental illness, including the famous delusion that he was made of glass.

Born in 1368, Charles VI became King of France at the tender age of 11. Initially, his reign showed promise, with the young king displaying military prowess and political acumen. However, everything changed in 1392 when Charles suffered his first episode of madness.

In August 1392, while on a military expedition, Charles suddenly drew his sword and began attacking his own men, killing several before he was subdued. This incident marked the beginning of Charles's lifelong struggle with mental illness.

Among Charles's most famous delusions was his belief that he was made of glass. This condition, now known as the "glass delusion," led to several peculiar behaviors; he refused to be touched, fearing he would shatter. Iron rods were sewn into his clothes to "protect" him from breaking and reportedly refused to sit down, fearing his glass buttocks would shatter.

Other Symptoms and Behaviors:

Charles's mental state fluctuated over the years. His symptoms included:

1. Periods of catatonia lasting months

2. Failure to recognize his wife and children

3. Running wildly through the palace until exhaustion

4. Bouts of severe depression

Charles's condition had profound implications for France. Various factions, including the king's brother Louis of Orleans and his cousin John the Fearless of Burgundy, vied for control during the king's periods of incapacity. The internal strife weakened France, allowing Henry V of England to invade and achieve a significant victory at Agincourt in 1415. In 1420, during a period of lucidity, Charles VI signed the Treaty of Troyes, disinheriting his son (the future Charles VII) in favor of Henry V of England.

Alwy M. Jones

The Haunting Tale of Joanna of Castile

In the annals of royal history, few stories are as tragic and captivating as that of Joanna of Castile, also known as Joanna the Mad. Her obsession with her deceased husband's body has intrigued historians and psychologists for centuries, offering a poignant glimpse into the intersection of power, love, and mental health in Renaissance Europe.

Joanna was born in 1479 to the Catholic Monarchs, Isabella I of Castile and Ferdinand II of Aragon. In 1496, she married Philip the Handsome, Duke of Burgundy, in a political alliance that would shape her destiny.

Philip died unexpectedly in 1506, possibly from typhoid fever. It was at this point that Joanna's behavior began to raise concerns. She refused to part with Philip's body, insisting on keeping it with her at all times.

She ordered the coffin to be opened regularly so she could embrace and kiss the corpse, traveling with the body across Spain, only moving at night and stopping at churches for services and sleeping next to the coffin.

Joanna's actions align with symptoms of prolonged, intense mourning that interferes with daily functioning. Philip's death occurred shortly after Joanna gave birth to their daughter Catherine, potentially triggering a severe mental health crisis. Some historians argue that Joanna showed signs of instability before Philip's death, possibly indicating schizophrenia or bipolar disorder.

Intense displays of grief and reverence for the dead were more accepted in medieval Catholic tradition. Her father, Ferdinand, used her behavior as justification to declare her unfit to rule, taking control of Castile. In 1509, Joanna was confined to the Santa Clara Convent in Tordesillas, where she remained for 46 years until her death.

Despite being the legal queen of Castile, Joanna was sidelined from actual rule. Her son, Charles V, became one of the most powerful monarchs in European history, ruling in her name.

Alwy M. Jones

Peter the Great's Razor-Sharp Reforms

In the annals of Russian history, few figures loom as large as Peter the Great. His reign, spanning from 1682 to 1725, was marked by sweeping reforms that sought to modernize and Westernize Russia. Among these reforms, one stands out as a particularly vivid example of Peter's forceful personality and his disregard for tradition; his mandate that all Russian men, with the exception of priests and peasants, shave their beards.

Upon returning from his tour of Western Europe, Peter was determined to remake Russia in the image of the countries he had visited. One of his first acts was to personally cut off the beards of his nobles at a reception. Shortly after, he instituted the beard tax; all men were required to shave their beards or pay a tax. Those who paid the tax were given a token to prove they had done so. The tax varied based on social status, with nobles paying the highest amount.

Peter saw beards as a symbol of Russia's backwardness and wanted to align Russian appearance with Western European norms. The policy was a clear demonstration of Peter's absolute authority over his subjects.

In the Russian Orthodox tradition, beards were seen as a sign of piety and masculinity. The Church viewed shaving as a sin.

The policy created visible distinctions between those who complied and those who resisted.

Alwy M. Jones

A Complex Intersection of Medical Ethics, Law, and Human Rights

In 2001, England witnessed the birth of conjoined twins Gracie and Rosie, a case that would go on to challenge medical, legal, and ethical boundaries.

Gracie and Rosie were born joined at the abdomen, sharing a fused liver and circulatory system. While both had their own hearts and lungs, Rosie's heart and lungs were significantly underdeveloped. As a result, she depended on Gracie's circulatory system to oxygenate her blood.

The medical team faced a challenging dilemma; if left unseparated, both twins would likely die within months due to the strain on Gracie's heart. Separation would almost certainly result in Rosie's death but would give Gracie a chance at a normal life. There was no medical intervention that could save both twins.

The case raised several unprecedented legal questions; could doctors legally perform a surgery that would inevitably lead to one twin's death to save the other? Did Rosie have a right to life that would prevent such a surgery? Could Gracie's right to life supersede Rosie's in this unique situation?

The case eventually reached the Court of Appeal, which ruled in favor of separation. The key points of the ruling included:

1. The doctrine of necessity: The court determined that the unique circumstances justified the surgery.

2. Best interests: The court considered the quality of life for both twins if left unseparated versus Gracie's potential for a normal life if separated.

3. Self-defense analogy: The court likened Rosie's dependence on Gracie to a form of invasion, justifying Gracie's right to be "freed" from this burden.

The case raised several ethical concerns:

1. The value of life: How to weigh the certain death of one against the potential life of the other.

2. Quality vs. quantity of life: Considering the twins' future quality of life in decision-making.

3. Medical intervention: The role and limits of medical intervention in such complex cases.

4. Parental rights: The extent to which parents can make life or death decisions for their children.

The case highlighted the unique legal status of conjoined twins:

1. Individual rights: Despite physical connection, each twin was considered a separate individual under the law.

2. Competing rights: The court had to balance the competing rights of two individuals whose lives were inextricably linked.

3. Precedent: The ruling set a precedent for future cases involving conjoined twins.

Alwy M. Jones

The Great Emu War of 1932

In the annals of unusual conflicts, few stand out quite like the Emu War of 1932. This peculiar episode in Australian history pitted the nation's military against an unlikely foe; large flightless birds native to the continent. What began as an attempt to control a burgeoning emu population quickly devolved into a series of comical and frustrating encounters that left the Australian military with a somewhat tarnished reputation and the Emus triumphant.

In the aftermath of World War I, many Australian soldiers were given land in Western Australia as part of a settlement scheme. These soldier-settlers turned to wheat farming, hoping to make a living in the state's marginal agricultural areas. However, their efforts were soon to be challenged by an unexpected adversary.

As the Great Depression hit in the early 1930s, wheat prices plummeted. To make matters worse, a horde of about 20,000 Emus began migrating from inland areas to the coastal wheat growing regions. These large birds, standing up to 6.2 feet tall and weighing up to 132 pounds, proved to be formidable agricultural pests. They devoured and damaged crops, leaving holes in fences that allowed rabbits to enter and cause further destruction.

The farmers, many of them ex-soldiers, appealed to the government for help. In response, the Minister of Defense, Sir George Pearce, agreed to send in the military. This decision was influenced by several factors; the farmers' status as war veterans. The potential for soldiers to gain experience in using machine guns in a mobile capacity. The fact that the Emus' feathers could be used for military uniforms

On November 2nd 1932, the operation began under the command of Major G.P.W. Meredith of the Seventh Heavy Battery of the Royal Australian Artillery. The force consisted of Meredith, two soldiers, two Lewis guns, and 10,000 rounds of ammunition.

The first encounter with the Emus proved to be a harbinger of the difficulties to come. As the soldiers prepared to open fire, the birds scattered, making it difficult to target them effectively. The heavy machine guns often jammed, further complicating the operation.

What the military had not anticipated was the Emus' remarkable ability to evade and withstand their attacks. The birds displayed several surprising tactical advantages; Emus can run at speeds up to 31 mph, making them difficult to target. The Emus moved in small groups, making large-scale attacks ineffective. The birds proved capable of withstanding multiple bullet wounds due to their thick feathers and strong muscles. The Emus seemed to quickly learn to stay out of range of the guns and to scatter when approached.

Despite several attempts, including an ambush near a local dam and the mounting of machine guns on trucks (which proved too slow to keep up with the emus), the military operation was largely unsuccessful. In one notable incident, a truck's axle was destroyed when the driver attempted to run down an Emu, leading to the loss of a valuable machine gun.

After about a month, and with only about 1,000 of the estimated 20,000 emus killed, the military withdrew. Major Meredith noted in his report, "If we had a military division with the bullet-carrying capacity of these birds, it would face any army in the world. They can face machine guns with the invulnerability of tanks."

The Emus had effectively "won" the war. The withdrawal of troops was seen as a victory for the birds, and the episode became something of an embarrassment for the Australian military. However, the farmers continued to face problems with the Emus.

In the following years, bounties were placed on Emus, and this more traditional method of pest control proved more effective over time. Between 1945 and 1960, around 284,700 Emus were killed under this bounty scheme.

A Landmark Conflict in Primate Behavior

The Gombe Chimpanzee War, also known as the Four-Year War, was a significant conflict that occurred among chimpanzees in Gombe Stream National Park, Tanzania, between 1974 and 1978. This event marked a pivotal moment in the study of primate behavior, challenging previous assumptions about chimpanzee social structures and providing unprecedented insights into the complexities of their communities. The conflict's documentation and analysis have had far-reaching implications for our understanding of primate sociology, evolutionary biology, and the roots of human warfare.

Gombe Stream National Park, located on the western border of Tanzania, has been a focal point for chimpanzee research since Jane Goodall established her field site there in 1960. The park's diverse ecosystem and relatively undisturbed chimpanzee population made it an ideal location for long-term behavioral studies.

Prior to the conflict, the Kasakela community was the primary group under observation. This community, initially comprising about 30 individuals, displayed a high degree of social cohesion and cooperation. Their daily activities, social interactions, and territorial patrols were meticulously recorded by Goodall and her team, providing a comprehensive baseline for understanding chimpanzee behavior in the wild.

Timeline of Events

1974: Tensions begin to rise within the Kasakela community, particularly among adult males.

1975: A group of six adult males, led by brothers Hugh and Charlie, begins to spend more time in the southern part of the Kasakela territory.

1976: The southern group, now known as the Kahama community, becomes increasingly isolated from the main Kasakela group.

1977: Violent encounters between the two groups escalate, with Kasakela males launching attacks into Kahama territory.

1978: The conflict reaches its peak, resulting in the extermination of the Kahama community and the reintegration of their territory into Kasakela lands.

Jane Goodall played a crucial role in observing and documenting the conflict. Her long-term presence and detailed field notes provided an unparalleled record of the events as they unfolded.

Significant chimpanzee individuals involved in the war included:

- Figan: The alpha male of the Kasakela community during most of the conflict.

- Humphrey: A high ranking Kasakela male known for his aggression.

- Hugh and Charlie: Brothers who led the breakaway Kahama group.

- Godi: The last surviving male of the Kahama community.

The primary cause of the conflict appears to have been competition for resources and territory. As the Kasakela community grew, social tensions increased, particularly among adult males vying for status and mating opportunities. The formation of the Kahama community likely resulted from these tensions, with a subset of males seeking to establish their own hierarchy and territory.

The conflict was characterized by violent raids conducted by Kasakela males into Kahama territory. These attacks often involved coordinated assaults on isolated Kahama individuals, resulting in severe injuries and fatalities. The violence observed during this period was unprecedented in its intensity and systematic nature, challenging previous notions of chimpanzee behavior.

The Gombe Chimpanzee War provided several key insights into chimpanzee behavior; it demonstrated that chimpanzees are capable of engaging in organized, inter-community violence. The conflict highlighted the importance of territory and resources in shaping chimpanzee social dynamics. The war revealed the complexity of chimpanzee political alliances and the potential for these to shift over time.

Long-term consequences included the expansion of the Kasakela territory and a period of increased vigilance and aggression towards neighboring communities.

The Mysterious Dancing Plague of 1518

In the summer of 1518, the city of Strasbourg, then part of the Holy Roman Empire, witnessed one of history's most bizarre and perplexing events; the dancing plague. This peculiar outbreak saw hundreds of people dancing uncontrollably for days on end, some until they collapsed from exhaustion or even died.

The dancing plague began in July 1518 when a woman known as Frau Troffea stepped into the street and began to dance fervently. Within a week, 34 others had joined her, and by the end of the month, the number had grown to 400. These people danced day and night, barely stopping to eat or sleep. Many dancers ultimately succumbed to heart attacks, strokes, or exhaustion.

Initially, local physicians attributed the phenomenon to "hot blood" and, strangely enough, recommended more dancing as a cure. The local authorities even went so far as to construct a wooden stage and hire musicians to keep the afflicted moving, believing this would eventually cure them.

Many modern researchers believe the dancing plague was a form of mass hysteria, now known as mass psychogenic illness. This theory suggests that extreme psychological stress can manifest in physical symptoms that spread through a population.

Some historians have proposed that the dancers may have consumed bread made from rye contaminated with ergot fungus, which can cause hallucinations and convulsions. However, ergot poisoning typically results in restricted blood flow to the limbs, making prolonged dancing unlikely.

The region had a history of similar dancing manias, often associated with St. Vitus, the patron saint of dancers. Some interpret the event as a form of religious ecstasy or a desperate appeal to the saint for intercession during troubled times.

The outbreak occurred during a period of extreme hardship, with famine, disease, and political strife afflicting the region. The dancing could have been a collective psychological response to these stressors.

To understand the dancing plague, it's crucial to consider the historical context of 16th century Strasbourg; the region had experienced several years of crop failures and food shortages. Outbreaks of syphilis and leprosy were common, causing fear and social upheaval.

Alwy M. Jones

A Sweet Escape or a Bitter Miscarriage of Justice?

The 1979 trial of Dan White for the assassinations of San Francisco Mayor George Moscone and Supervisor Harvey Milk stands as one of the most controversial cases in American legal history. At the heart of this controversy lies the infamous "Twinkie Defense," a strategy that has since become synonymous with dubious legal arguments.

The "Twinkie Defense" was not, as popularly believed, a claim that Twinkies directly caused White's actions. Rather, the defense argued that White's consumption of junk food, including Twinkies, was evidence of his depression and diminished capacity. Defense psychiatrist Martin Blinder testified that White's shift from a health conscious diet to one high in sugar and carbohydrates was indicative of serious depression, which impaired his judgment.

This argument was part of a broader diminished capacity defense, which sought to portray White as a man struggling with depression and operating under extreme emotional distress. The defense team aimed to have White's charges reduced from first-degree murder to voluntary manslaughter by demonstrating that he lacked the mental state required for premeditation.

The strategy proved surprisingly effective. White was convicted of voluntary manslaughter rather than first-degree murder, receiving a sentence of just seven years and eight months. This outcome sparked outrage in San Francisco, particularly among the LGBTQ+ community, who viewed it as a gross injustice for the murder of Harvey Milk, one of the first openly gay elected officials in the United States.

The success of the "Twinkie Defense" can be attributed to several factors. Firstly, it played into existing stereotypes and misconceptions about mental health. The idea that depression could manifest in dietary changes was not well understood by the general public or the jury. Secondly, the defense team skillfully used expert testimony to lend credibility to their argument. Lastly, the prosecution's failure to effectively counter this narrative allowed it to gain traction.

However, the "Twinkie Defense" has been widely criticized and often misrepresented. Legal scholars argue that its success was more due to effective overall strategy by the defense team and mistakes by the prosecution than the persuasiveness of the junk food argument itself. As noted by law professor Robert Weisberg, "It was a good insanity defense. It's ridiculous to call it the Twinkie defense."

The public perception of the "Twinkie Defense" has had lasting implications for the legal system. It has become a symbol of questionable defense strategies and has led to increased scrutiny of expert testimony in trials. In California, the case directly led to the abolition of the diminished capacity defense in 1982.

Critics argue that the success of such a defense undermines the integrity of the legal system. They contend that it opens the door for defendants to escape justice by presenting pseudo-scientific arguments. As legal analyst Jeffrey Toobin noted, "The Twinkie Defense became shorthand for a legal system that had gone off the rails."

On the other hand, proponents of mental health awareness argue that the case, despite its flaws, highlighted the need for a more nuanced understanding of mental illness in the legal system. They contend that while the specific argument about Twinkies was flawed, the underlying principle of considering mental state in criminal cases is valid.

Alwy M. Jones

The Unflinching Horror of Buck Breaking

Hidden beneath the surface of American chattel slavery lurked a depravity so profound it defies easy comprehension; Buck Breaking. This barbaric practice wasn't just about punishment; it was a calculated act of sexual violence meticulously designed to dismantle the physical and psychological spirit of enslaved men.

Buck breaking, also known as "Negro-breaking" or "opening the way," targeted newly acquired slaves, particularly those deemed strong or defiant. The process often began with public humiliation and physical beatings, stripping the victim of any shred of dignity. Then came the core element; the rape of the enslaved man, most often perpetrated by a white male overseer or the slave owner himself.

This wasn't just about satisfying a perverse desire. Buck breaking served a multitude of sinister purposes. It was a brutal assertion of dominance, a way to demonstrate to the entire enslaved population that no man, regardless of strength, was safe from the whims of their white oppressors. It was a tactic to extinguish any spark of resistance, turning a potentially rebellious man into a broken, submissive shell. This act of sexual violence redefined enslaved men as not just property, but objects of white male desire, further blurring the lines of their humanity.

The horror didn't stop there. Historical accounts point to the existence of so called "sex farms," collaborations between slave owners where enslaved men were systematically raped and forced into sexual acts for the collective gratification of the white enslavers. These accounts, though chilling, offer a glimpse into the depths of depravity that the institution of slavery fostered.

The psychological impact of buck breaking on the enslaved men was catastrophic. Shame, fear, and a sense of utter powerlessness became their constant companions. Many suffered from long-term physical injuries and sexually transmitted diseases. Suicide attempts and desperate escapes were likely responses to this unimaginable trauma.

Understanding the historical context of buck breaking is crucial. It wasn't an anomaly; it was a brutal tool deliberately employed to maintain the power structure of slavery. Southern slave codes rarely addressed sexual violence against slaves, implicitly condoning it. The prevailing racist ideology of the time dehumanized Black people, making them objects to be used and abused at will.

Buck breaking serves as a stark reminder of the dark underbelly of American history. While its legacy is often obscured, its impact on enslaved men and the institution of slavery as a whole is undeniable. Unflinchingly confronting these historical atrocities is essential to ensure such horrors are never repeated.

Alwy M. Jones

A Legal Loophole

In a surprising anomaly, four states in the United States; New Mexico, West Virginia, Hawaii, and Wyoming lack specific laws prohibiting bestiality. This legal grey area has sparked concern among animal rights advocates and legal experts, raising questions about animal welfare and potential public safety risks.

While all states have animal cruelty laws, these typically focus on preventing physical harm or neglect. Bestiality, however, involves a complex issue of consent and potential psychological trauma for the animal. Without specific legislation targeting bestiality, prosecution becomes difficult.

Animal rights groups argue that bestiality is inherently cruel and exploitative. Animals cannot consent to sexual acts, and the experience can cause physical injury and significant psychological distress. Beyond immediate harm, there's a concern about potential zoonotic diseases, illnesses transmissible between animals and humans. Additionally, some experts point to a possible link between bestiality and other forms of animal cruelty or even child sexual abuse.

Calls for reform are growing in these four states. Proposed legislation typically classifies bestiality as a misdemeanor or felony, depending on the severity of the act and potential harm caused to the animal. Additionally, such laws often include mandatory reporting requirements for suspected cases.

The path to reform, however, can be challenging. Public discomfort with the topic and potential legal challenges can create hurdles for legislators. However, advocates are highlighting the importance of animal welfare and the need for legal clarity in deterring this practice.

New Mexico: In 2023, a bill was introduced to make bestiality a crime. The bill's status is currently unclear.

West Virginia: No legislation has been proposed yet, but animal welfare groups are pushing for action.

Hawaii: Similar to New Mexico, a 2021 bill aiming to criminalize bestiality is under consideration.

Wyoming: Calls for reform are ongoing, with no official legislative effort yet.

Alwy M. Jones

Unveiling the Myth of Catherine the Great and Her Horse

Catherine the Great, Empress of Russia from 1762 to 1796, remains a captivating figure. Her reign ushered in a golden age of Russian power and culture, but whispers of scandal have clung to her reputation for centuries. One particularly enduring rumor centers on her alleged sexual relationship with a horse.

The earliest mention of Catherine and the horse appears in French pamphlets published in the late 18th century, a time rife with political tensions between Russia and France. These pamphlets were known for their salacious content and targeted Catherine's reputation as a powerful and independent woman.

Catherine was known for her voracious appetite for knowledge and her patronage of the arts. She also had a number of well documented romantic relationships, most notably with Grigory Potemkin, a powerful advisor. While some of these relationships were unconventional, there's no evidence to suggest anything as outlandish as the horse story.

Catherine was a woman who defied expectations. She wielded power in a male dominated world, and her personal life was no different. This, combined with the political climate of the time, made her a ripe target for outlandish rumors.

Alwy M. Jones

Radium Therapy in the Early 20th Century

In the early 20th century, a luminous element captured the imagination of scientists, medical professionals, and the general public alike. Radium, discovered by Marie and Pierre Curie in 1898, was heralded as a miraculous substance with seemingly limitless potential. This led to the widespread adoption of radium therapy, a practice that would have far-reaching and often tragic consequences.

Following its discovery, radium quickly gained a reputation as a cure-all. Its ability to emit energy in the form of radiation was seen as a source of vitality and health. This perception was fueled by limited scientific understanding and aggressive marketing campaigns that promoted radium as a panacea for various ailments.

Perhaps the most popular method of consuming radium was through drinking water infused with the element. Products like "Radithor" and "Radiumscope" allowed people to add radium to their drinking water at home. Some spas even offered radium baths, promising rejuvenation and vitality.

Consumers could purchase a range of radioactive products, including watch dials, jewelry, and even clothing items. These were marketed as having health promoting properties due to their constant emission of radiation.

In medical settings, some practitioners administered radium injections directly into patients' bodies, believing it could treat various conditions from arthritis to cancer.

Beauty products containing radium were popular, with claims of improving skin health and providing a "healthy glow."

Unknown to its proponents, radium therapy was causing severe damage to those exposed to it. Radium is a radioactive element that decays over time, releasing alpha, beta, and gamma radiation. These types of radiation can cause significant harm to living tissues. While it cannot penetrate the skin, it is extremely dangerous if ingested or inhaled, causing severe internal damage. Beta radiation can penetrate skin and cause burns and cellular damage. Gamma radiation is the most penetrating form, capable of causing widespread cellular damage throughout the body.

The effects of radiation exposure include; DNA damage leading to mutations and cancer, destruction of bone marrow, leading to anemia and immunodeficiency, necrosis of soft tissues and bone degradation.

One of the most infamous cases highlighting the dangers of radium exposure is that of the "Radium Girls." In the 1920s, young women were employed to paint watch dials with radium based luminous paint. They were instructed to paint their brushes with their lips, inadvertently ingesting small amounts of radium with each stroke.

Many of these women later developed severe health issues, including; anemia, bone fractures, necrosis of the jaw (dubbed "radium jaw") and various forms of cancer.

The plight of the Radium Girls eventually led to increased awareness of radium's dangers and improvements in workplace safety standards. However, it came at a tremendous cost to the health and lives of these workers.

As cases of radiation poisoning became more prevalent and better understood, the perception of radium therapy began to shift. By the 1930s and 1940s, the scientific community was becoming increasingly aware of the long-term effects of radiation exposure.

The Toxic Cure

For centuries, mercury held a prominent place in the medical arsenal, revered for its supposed curative properties despite its insidious toxicity. This heavy metal's use in medicine, particularly in the treatment of syphilis, serves as a stark reminder of the dangers inherent in medical practices not grounded in scientific understanding.

The use of mercury in medicine dates back to ancient civilizations, including China and India. In Western medicine, it gained particular prominence during the Renaissance and remained a common treatment well into the 20th century. Its use was based on the humoral theory of medicine, which posited that illnesses resulted from an imbalance of bodily fluids. Mercury was believed to restore this balance by promoting the expulsion of "bad humors" through increased salivation, urination, and sweating.

Mercury found its most infamous application in the treatment of syphilis, a sexually transmitted infection caused by the bacterium Treponema pallidum. The disease, which first appeared in Europe in the late 15th century, quickly became a widespread and devastating epidemic.

Patients were exposed to mercury vapors in enclosed "sweating tubs." This method often led to severe respiratory issues and death. Mercury based ointments were applied directly to syphilitic sores or rubbed into the skin. Mercury compounds were administered orally in the form of pills or liquids. In later periods, mercury compounds were sometimes injected directly into the body.

The treatment regimen was often long and grueling, lasting months or even years. A common saying of the time reflected the harsh nature of mercury treatment; "A night with Venus, a lifetime with Mercury."

While mercury did have some effect on the symptoms of syphilis, its use came at a tremendous cost to patients' health; neurological damage, tremors, memory loss, cognitive impairment, kidney failure, severe dental problems and loss of teeth, skin rashes and ulcerations, excessive salivation and oral ulcers and gastrointestinal issues.

Ironically, many of these symptoms mimicked or exacerbated the tertiary stage of syphilis, making it difficult to distinguish between the effects of the disease and its treatment.

Alwy M. Jones

The Controversial Legacy of Malaria Therapy

In the annals of medical history, few treatments have been as paradoxical and controversial as Julius Wagner-Jauregg's malaria therapy for syphilis. This unconventional approach, developed in the 1920s, intentionally infected patients with a potentially deadly disease to treat another, earning its creator both accolades and criticism.

In the early 20th century, neurosyphilis, the late stage form of syphilis affecting the nervous system was a devastating and common condition. With limited treatment options available, the medical community was desperate for new approaches to combat this debilitating disease.

Julius Wagner-Jauregg, an Austrian psychiatrist, had long been interested in the relationship between fever and mental illness. His observations of patients with psychiatric symptoms improving after experiencing high fevers led him to explore the therapeutic potential of artificially induced fever.

Wagner-Jauregg's breakthrough came in 1917 when he successfully treated a patient suffering from neurosyphilis by intentionally infecting him with malaria. The rationale behind this approach was based on several key observations; high body temperatures were known to inhibit the growth of certain bacteria, including Treponema pallidum, the causative agent of syphilis. Among fever inducing diseases, malaria was chosen for its relatively predictable fever cycles and the availability of quinine as a treatment. Existing treatments for neurosyphilis, such as mercury compounds, were often ineffective and highly toxic.

Patients were infected with Plasmodium vivax, a less lethal strain of the malaria parasite, often through blood transfusion from an infected individual or mosquito bites. Patients would experience recurring high fevers, often reaching 40-41°C (104-106°F). Medical staff closely monitored patients through 8-10 fever cycles, typically lasting about 6-8 weeks. Once the desired number of fever cycles was achieved, patients were treated with quinine to cure the malaria. Patients were then monitored for improvements in their syphilis symptoms.

The primary mechanism behind malaria therapy was the induction of high fever. This elevated body temperature was believed to create an inhospitable environment for the syphilis-causing bacteria. Additionally, the fever was thought to stimulate the body's immune response, potentially enhancing its ability to fight off the syphilis infection.

Alwy M. Jones

A Dark Chapter in Psychiatric Treatment

Insulin Coma Therapy (ICT), also known as Insulin Shock Therapy, represents one of the most controversial and dangerous treatments in the history of psychiatry. Developed in the 1930s and widely used until the 1960s, this therapy exemplifies the desperate measures taken in early attempts to treat severe mental illnesses, particularly schizophrenia.

Insulin Coma Therapy was first introduced in 1933 by Austrian-American psychiatrist Manfred Sakel. Sakel stumbled upon the idea while using small doses of insulin to treat drug addicts. He noticed that patients who accidentally received overdoses of insulin, resulting in comas, showed improvements in their mental states upon recovery.

The therapy quickly gained popularity in psychiatric institutions across Europe and North America. It was seen as a revolutionary treatment for schizophrenia, a condition for which there were few effective therapies at the time.

The basic principle of Insulin Coma Therapy involved administering large doses of insulin to patients, inducing a hypoglycemic state that led to coma. The procedure typically followed; patients being required to fast overnight. Large doses of insulin were injected, often starting at 15-20 units and increasing daily. Patients were closely observed as they progressed through stages of hypoglycemia, including sweating, restlessness, and unconsciousness. The insulin dose was increased until the patient entered a coma, typically lasting 15-60 minutes. Patients were revived using glucose solutions, either orally or intravenously. This process was repeated multiple times per week for several weeks or months.

The exact mechanism by which Insulin Coma Therapy was thought to improve psychiatric symptoms remains unclear. Several theories were proposed;

1. "Therapeutic Shock": It was believed that the shock of the coma could somehow reset aberrant brain functions.

2. Neuroplasticity: Some theorized that the repeated comas stimulated the growth of new neural pathways.

3. Psychological Impact: The intensive care required during treatment was thought to have a beneficial psychological effect on patients.

4. Metabolic Theory: Changes in brain metabolism during hypoglycemia were believed to alter brain chemistry positively.

Risks and Mortality

Insulin Coma Therapy was an extremely dangerous procedure with a high mortality rate. Estimates suggest that about 1-2% of patients died as a direct result of the treatment.

1. Prolonged Coma: Difficulty in reviving patients from insulin-induced comas.

2. Brain Damage: Hypoglycemia could cause irreversible neurological damage.

3. Seizures: Severe hypoglycemia often led to seizures.

4. Cardiovascular Complications: Heart problems were common due to the stress placed on the body.

5. Weight Gain: Patients often experienced significant weight gain due to the glucose administrations.

Alwy M. Jones

The Medical History of George Washington

George Washington, the first President of the United States and a pivotal figure in American history, suffered from various health issues throughout his life.

From a young age, Washington faced several health challenges. He survived smallpox at the age of 19 during a trip to Barbados in 1751, which left him with facial scars but also provided him with immunity during later outbreaks.

Washington suffered from recurring bouts of malaria and dysentery, common afflictions in colonial America. These diseases caused periodic debilitation and may have contributed to his overall health decline over time.

Perhaps one of Washington's most well-known health problems was his dental issues. By the time he became president, he had only ONE natural tooth remaining. He wore dentures made from various materials, including human teeth, ivory, and metal. These dental problems caused him considerable pain and difficulty eating and speaking.

One of the most intriguing aspects of Washington's medical history is the question of his infertility. While Washington and his wife Martha raised her two children from a previous marriage and later their grandchildren, the couple never had biological children together.

Historical evidence and modern medical analysis suggest that Washington may have suffered from tuberculous epididymitis, a form of genitourinary tuberculosis that can cause infertility in men.

Symptoms and Effects of Tuberculous Epididymitis:

1. Swelling and pain in the testicles

2. Difficulty urinating

3. Infertility due to blockage of sperm ducts

4. General symptoms of tuberculosis (fever, weight loss, fatigue)

Tuberculosis was widespread in 18th century America, and its various forms were not well understood. The genitourinary form of the disease was particularly challenging to diagnose and treat.

Alwy M. Jones

The Paradoxical History of Asthma Cigarettes

In the annals of medical history, few treatments seem as counterintuitive as prescribing cigarettes to relieve asthma symptoms. Yet, for much of the 19th and early 20th centuries, this practice was not only common but enthusiastically endorsed by many physicians. The story of asthma cigarettes serves as a stark reminder of how medical understanding evolves and the importance of evidence based medicine.

Asthma cigarettes, typically containing stramonium (a plant of the nightshade family) and sometimes cannabis, gained popularity in the mid-19th century. The medical rationale behind their use was based on the bronchodilating effects of these substances. When inhaled, they were thought to relax the smooth muscles of the airways, providing relief from asthma symptoms.

Dr. Henry Hyde Salter, a prominent 19th century physician, wrote in his 1860 treatise "On Asthma: Its Pathology and Treatment":

"The fumes of stramonium have a power of relaxing spasm of the bronchial tubes... and of thus giving relief in asthma that is almost magical."

This endorsement from a respected medical authority lent credibility to the practice, leading to widespread adoption.

The active compounds in stramonium, particularly atropine and scopolamine, are anticholinergic agents that can indeed cause bronchodilation. Similarly, the cannabinoids in cannabis have some anti-inflammatory and bronchodilating properties. Patients often reported immediate relief from their asthma symptoms after smoking these cigarettes.

Dr. William Osler, often called the "Father of Modern Medicine," recommended cannabis for asthma in his 1892 textbook "The Principles and Practice of Medicine":

"The cigarettes made from stramonium leaves or from cubebs sometimes give relief... Inhalations of the fumes of burning nitre paper or stramonium leaves are also useful."

The irony of prescribing smoking for a respiratory condition cannot be overstated. While the immediate bronchodilating effects might have provided temporary relief, the long-term consequences of smoking were not yet fully understood.

Alwy M. Jones

Sky Burial

In the high altitude plateaus of Tibet, a unique and profound funerary practice known as "sky burial" or "jhator" has been performed for centuries. This ritual, deeply rooted in Tibetan Buddhist traditions, offers a stark contrast to Western burial practices and provides fascinating insights into Tibetan views on death, impermanence, and the relationship between humans and nature.

Sky burial is more than just a method of corpse disposal; it is a ritual that embodies core Tibetan Buddhist principles; the practice emphasizes the temporary nature of the physical body. Offering one's body to feed other creatures is considered a final act of compassion. Sky burial is believed to accumulate positive karma for the deceased. The ritual symbolizes the continuous cycle of birth, death, and rebirth.

The sky burial ritual involves several stages, each imbued with spiritual significance; the body is usually kept untouched for three days after death, during which time prayers are recited. The corpse is then cleaned and wrapped in white cloth. The body is transported to a designated sky burial site, typically located on a high mountaintop. Family members may accompany the body, though they usually do not witness the actual ritual. A rogyapa (body-breaker) performs the ritual, which begins at dawn. The body is unwrapped and positioned in a specific manner. Incense is burned, and prayers are chanted to summon vultures, considered sacred birds.

The rogyapa skillfully dismembers the body using specialized tools. Flesh is cut into small pieces and scattered for the vultures to consume. Bones are ground into a powder, mixed with barley flour and butter, and also offered to the birds.

The ritual is considered complete when the vultures have consumed all the remains. Any leftover bones or clothing are burned.

Alwy M. Jones

The Controversial Practice of Widow Immolation in India

Sati, the practice of widow immolation on her husband's funeral pyre, stands as one of the most controversial and debated customs in Indian history. This ancient ritual, steeped in complex cultural and religious beliefs, has been both revered as the ultimate act of wifely devotion and condemned as a brutal form of oppression.

The origins of Sati are disputed, with some scholars tracing it back to the 4th century BCE, while others argue for a later emergence. The practice gained prominence during the medieval period, particularly in regions of North India. Historical records indicate that Sati was most prevalent among the ruling and warrior castes, though it was not uniformly practiced across all regions and communities of India.

The first recorded ban on Sati was issued by Mughal Emperor Akbar in the late 16th century. However, the practice continued, with varying degrees of prevalence, until the British colonial period. The British East India Company initially adopted a non-interventionist stance, viewing Sati as a religious practice. This changed in 1829 when Governor General William Bentinck, influenced by Indian reformers like Raja Ram Mohan Roy, officially banned Sati in Company ruled territories.

Sati was deeply rooted in cultural and religious beliefs about marriage, devotion, and the afterlife. It was often portrayed as a voluntary act of ultimate devotion, where a widow would choose to join her husband in death rather than face the hardships of widowhood in a patriarchal society. The act was associated with purity, sacrifice, and spiritual merit.

In Hindu mythology, Sati is the name of Lord Shiva's first wife, who immolated herself to protest her father's insult to her husband. This mythological connection lent divine sanction to the practice in the eyes of its proponents.

The cultural significance of Sati extended beyond the act itself. Sati-stones, memorial stones erected to commemorate women who performed Sati, became objects of worship in some communities. The glorification of Sati in folklore, literature, and art further embedded it in the cultural consciousness.

The Sharpening of the Soul

Known as "metatah" or "mepandes" in the local language, tooth filing is a rite of passage deeply rooted in Balinese Hindu tradition. It's a practice that dates back centuries, intertwining spiritual beliefs with physical transformation. The significance of the ritual lies in its symbolic power to tame the "six evils" that reside within every human: lust, greed, wrath, pride, jealousy, and intoxication. These negative traits, it is believed, are embodied in the canine teeth, the sharp, animalistic remnants of our baser nature. By filing these teeth, the Balinese believe they are not just altering their physical appearance, but refining their very souls.

The ritual begins with prayers and blessings, invoking the gods to watch over the proceedings. The sangging approaches with his tools, a small file and a piece of sugarcane. The sugarcane, will be placed between her teeth to protect her tongue and to catch the filings, which will later be buried in a special ceremony.

Each gentle scrape of the file against the teeth is a step towards balance, towards harmony between her physical and spiritual selves. The process is not painful, but it is intense.

Each person present is reminded of their own passage through this ritual, of the ongoing process of refining one's character and controlling one's baser instincts.

Alwy M. Jones

The Bound Lotus

Foot binding, a practice that spanned nearly a thousand years of Chinese history, stands as one of the most extreme examples of body modification for the sake of beauty and social status.

Foot binding is believed to have originated in the late Tang Dynasty (618-907 CE), possibly introduced by a court dancer named Yao Niang. The practice gained popularity during the Song Dynasty (960-1279 CE) and reached its peak during the Ming (1368-1644 CE) and Qing (1644-1911 CE) dynasties. Initially confined to the upper classes, foot binding gradually spread to all social strata, becoming a mark of Han Chinese identity.

The process of foot binding typically began when a girl was between 4 and 9 years old. It involved; breaking the arch of the foot, bending the toes under the sole, wrapping the foot tightly with long strips of cloth

This process was repeated regularly, with increasingly tighter bindings, resulting in severely deformed feet, ideally no longer than 3-4 inches (7.5-10 cm), broken bones and atrophied muscles. Reduced circulation leading to frequent infections, difficulty walking and balance issues, lifelong pain and limited mobility

The desired shape, known as the "golden lotus," was achieved through years of painful binding. The ideal bound foot was approximately 3 inches long

Foot binding was deeply intertwined with notions of beauty, status, and morality in traditional Chinese society. Small feet were considered the height of feminine beauty and grace. Bound feet were a prerequisite for marriage into wealthy families. The practice was associated with Confucian ideals of female chastity and obedience. Women with bound feet were confined to the domestic sphere, reinforcing gender roles.

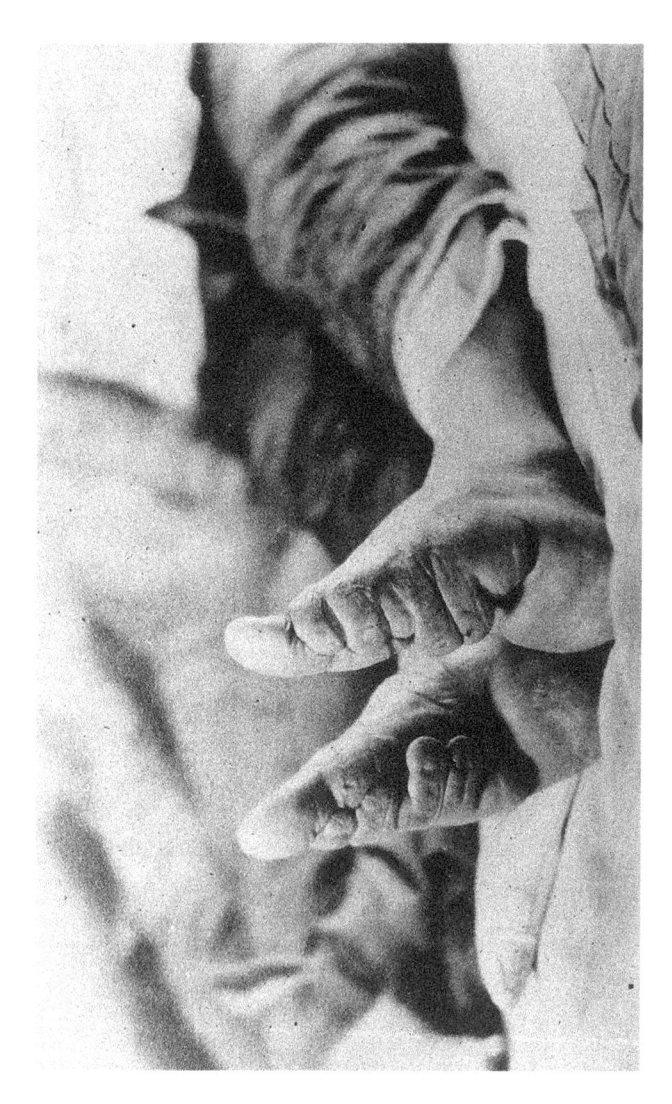

- Feet of a Chinese woman, showing the effect of foot-binding

Alwy M. Jones

The Extraordinary Case of Ahmed al-Masri

In the winding streets of Sana'a, Yemen's ancient capital, is Ahmed al-Masri, a 35 year old shopkeeper whose remarkable anatomy captured international attention. Ahmed is not your average man, he possesses four fully functioning kidneys, a medical rarity that has both baffled doctors and tested his faith.

He first discovered his condition during a routine medical check-up. Ahmed's refusal to sell his extra kidneys was rooted deeply in his religious beliefs. Despite the medical community's interest, Ahmed refused extensive testing, allowing only basic scans and blood work. Indeed, Ahmed reports no health issues related to his unique anatomy.

Four-kidney individuals are extremely rare, with only a few documented cases worldwide. The condition is often associated with genetic mutations or developmental abnormalities.

Examples:

Wang Kailian: A Chinese man who had one of his four kidneys removed due to infection. His case was reported in 2016.

Slawomir Peszko: A Polish professional footballer who has four kidneys, a result of a genetic condition called duplex kidneys.

Laura Moon: A British teenager who was discovered to have four kidneys in 2008. Her case was unusual in that each of her kidneys had two fully functioning systems.

Surinder Kumar Sahoo: An Indian man who underwent three kidney transplants and now has four kidneys. His case was reported in 2017.

Patsy Doherty: An Irish man who had four kidneys, three of which failed, and the fourth was on its way to failing, requiring multiple transplants.

Alwy M. Jones

The Shocking Case of a Scalpel Left Behind

In a case that has sent shockwaves through Brazil's medical community and beyond, 52 year old Maria Santos has lived with a chilling secret for over two decades, a surgical scalpel left inside her body during a caesarean section 23 years prior.

For years she felt this stabbing pain, doctors told her it was normal, that it was just adhesions from the C-section. The truth came to light when Maria, plagued by increasingly severe abdominal pain, underwent an X-ray at a local clinic in Sao Paulo. The image revealed a startling sight; a clearly defined surgical scalpel nestled in her abdomen.

The scalpel, measuring approximately 11 centimeters, had somehow been overlooked during the closure of Maria's C-section incision in 1998. More astounding still is that it remained undetected through numerous medical examinations over the years.

Indeed, while surgical items being left inside patients is not unheard of, with an estimated 1,500 such cases occurring annually worldwide, the length of time and the nature of the item in Maria's case make it particularly egregious.

Gold Injections

Gold injections, also known as gold therapy or chrysotherapy, involve injecting gold salts into the body. This treatment has been used for decades, primarily for rheumatoid arthritis. The gold compounds are thought to have anti-inflammatory properties that can help reduce joint swelling and pain.

Gold therapy can be effective for some patients, particularly those with rheumatoid arthritis who haven't responded well to other treatments. Studies have shown that it can reduce inflammation and slow joint damage in some cases. However, it's important to note that the response varies greatly between individuals.

One potential advantage is its long-lasting effect. Unlike some medications that need to be taken daily, gold injections are typically administered weekly or monthly, and their effects can persist for some time. Additionally, for patients who can't tolerate or haven't responded to other disease modifying antirheumatic drugs (DMARDs), gold can be an alternative option."

Yes, there are potential side effects to consider. These can range from mild skin rashes to more serious issues like kidney problems or blood disorders. Because of these risks, patients are closely monitored, receiving gold therapy with regular blood and urine tests.

Typically gold therapy is considered for patients with moderate to severe rheumatoid arthritis who haven't responded well to other treatments. Careful evaluation of each patient's medical history, current health status, and potential risk factors before the treatment is recommended.

While gold therapy was once a mainstay of rheumatoid arthritis treatment, it's used less frequently now due to the development of newer, often more effective, and sometimes safer medications. Biologic drugs and newer DMARDs have largely replaced gold as first-line treatments. However, gold therapy remains a viable option for some patients, particularly when other treatments have failed."

Alwy M. Jones

Baring It All

In a city known for its liberal attitudes, Amsterdam has taken fitness to a bold new frontier. At "Naaktfit" (literally "Naked Fit"), a gym in the heart of the Dutch capital, members are shedding more than just calories, they're shedding their clothes.

The concept, brainchild of fitness entrepreneur Jan de Vries, aims to promote body positivity and a back to basics approach to exercise. "We're born naked, why not exercise naked?" de Vries explains. "It's about reconnecting with our bodies in the most natural state."

The gym has strict hygiene protocols. Participants must bring their own towels to place on equipment, and the facility is cleaned rigorously between sessions. Photography is strictly forbidden, and new members undergo an induction process to ensure they understand the rules and etiquette.

The argument is while it may seem extreme, this approach can be beneficial for some individuals in overcoming body shame and developing a healthier relationship with their physical selves.

The legal aspects of naked gyms are complex. Dutch law allows for nudity in designated areas, and Naaktfit operates within these parameters. However, the gym has faced challenges in advertising and social media presence due to nudity restrictions on various platforms.

Alwy M. Jones

The Netherlands has a history of body acceptance, from nude beaches to open attitudes about sex education. This gym is an extension of that cultural mindset.

Alwy M. Jones

The Synesthetic World of Wassily Kandinsky

"Synaesthesia is a neurological trait where stimulation in one sensory or cognitive pathway leads to involuntary experiences in another. For example, some people might see colors when they hear music or taste flavors when they read words."

Wassily Kandinsky, the pioneering abstract artist, is believed to have experienced this unique sensory blending, particularly in the form of color sound synaesthesia. Kandinsky reportedly saw colors when he heard music and heard sounds when he saw colors. This dual sensory experience profoundly influenced his artistic style and theory.

For a synesthete like Kandinsky, the world is inherently more interconnected, colors aren't just visual experiences but carry auditory or even emotional weight. This can lead to incredibly rich and complex artistic expressions.

Synesthetes often report that their additional sensory experiences provide inspiration and novel associations. For Kandinsky, it allowed him to pioneer abstract art by translating music's non-representational nature into visual form.

Not all synesthetes become artists, and not all artists are synesthetes. While synaesthesia can certainly contribute to unique creative perspectives, it's not a guarantee of artistic talent. What's crucial is how an individual harnesses and expresses their perceptual experiences.

The influence of synaesthesia extends beyond visual art. In music, composers like Alexander Scriabin and Olivier Messiaen have created works directly inspired by their synesthetic experiences. In literature, Vladimir Nabokov's vivid descriptions were influenced by his grapheme color synaesthesia.

Alwy M. Jones

A Controversial Chapter in Medical History

The practice of monkey testicle transplantation, a controversial and now discredited medical procedure, represents a fascinating yet troubling chapter in the history of medical experimentation.

The concept of transplanting animal testicles into humans emerged in the late 19th and early 20th centuries, driven by the growing field of endocrinology and the search for "rejuvenation" treatments. The most prominent figure associated with this practice was Dr. Serge Voronoff, a French surgeon of Russian origin.

Voronoff's work was influenced by the contemporary understanding of hormones and their effects on the body. He hypothesized that transplanting testicular tissue from younger animals into aging humans could restore vitality, increase longevity, and treat various age related conditions.

The typical procedure involved harvesting testicles from young monkeys (usually chimpanzees or baboons), slicing the tissue into thin grafts and surgically implanting these grafts into the patient's scrotum or abdominal wall.

Voronoff claimed that the monkey tissue would fuse with the human tissue, releasing hormones that would rejuvenate the patient.

Proponents of the procedure claimed numerous benefits:

1. Increased physical strength and stamina

2. Enhanced mental acuity

3. Improved sexual function

4. Reversal of aging processes

5. Treatment of conditions like dementia and arthritis

The scientific basis for these transplants was rooted in the emerging understanding of hormones, particularly testosterone. Researchers of the time believed that introducing young, hormone producing tissue could compensate for the decline in hormone production associated with aging.

While many of the reported "successes" were anecdotal, some notable cases include:

1. Voronoff himself claimed to have performed over 500 such transplants, reporting significant improvements in his patients.

2. Several high profile individuals, including wealthy businessmen and even some politicians, reportedly underwent the procedure.

The procedure carried significant risks; the risk of zoonotic diseases transferring from monkeys to humans was high, the human immune system often rejected the foreign tissue, the grafts could potentially produce hormones in unpredictable ways and the procedure could have significant psychological impacts on patients.

Alwy M. Jones

Breakfast During the Middle Ages

During the Middle Ages (5th to 15th century), the practice of giving children beer for breakfast was indeed common in parts of Europe, particularly in England and Northern Europe. This custom might seem shocking by today's standards, but it's important to understand the context of the time.

Clean drinking water was scarce in medieval times. Rivers and wells were often contaminated with sewage and pathogens. The brewing process for beer involved boiling, which killed many harmful microorganisms, making it safer to drink than water. Medieval beer, often called "small beer," was typically low in alcohol content (around 1-3%). It provided calories, carbohydrates, and some vitamins, serving as a source of nutrition in a time when food scarcity was common.

Alcohol consumption was deeply ingrained in medieval society, with beer and ale considered staple beverages for all ages. The concept of childhood as we understand it today didn't exist; children were often treated as small adults. Beer had a longer shelf life than many other foods and drinks, making it a reliable source of sustenance.

Alwy M. Jones

Catholic Church's Decision to Ban Sausages

This prohibition reflects the complex relationship between emerging Christianity and existing pagan traditions in the early centuries of the Common Era.

Early Christianity (1st - 4th centuries CE); the early Church was working to establish its identity and distinguish itself from pagan religions. There was a concerted effort to distance Christian practices from those associated with pagan rituals and festivals.

Many pagan festivals involved feasting, with specific foods playing important roles in rituals. Sausages were often featured in these celebrations, particularly in Roman and Germanic traditions.

The ban on sausages is often attributed to the early 4th century, it's believed to have been implemented under Emperor Constantine, who legalized Christianity in the Roman Empire.

Sausages were associated with pagan fertility rituals and festivals honoring gods like Lupercus. The Church viewed these associations as incompatible with Christian teachings and morality.

The phallic shape of sausages was seen as a symbol of lust and excess, contrary to Christian ideals of temperance and chastity.

Banning sausages was part of a broader effort to create a distinct Christian culture separate from pagan traditions. It served as a visible way for Christians to differentiate themselves from their pagan neighbors.

The Church began to exert influence over dietary habits as a means of spiritual discipline. This laid the groundwork for later practices like fasting and abstinence from certain foods during religious observances.

The sausage ban was one of many measures aimed at suppressing pagan customs and rituals. It reflected the Church's strategy of replacing pagan holidays with Christian ones and redefining cultural practices.

Alwy M. Jones

Birds of a Feather Tweet Together

In a groundbreaking study published in the journal "Avian Communication," a team of phonetics experts and ornithologists have uncovered evidence that birds of the same species can develop distinct regional accents, much like humans do.

The use of advanced sound analysis software to compare recordings of great tits (Parus major) from different regions across Europe. What was astounding was the subtle but consistent differences in pitch, rhythm, and tonal quality that corresponded to geographic locations. The team collected over 1,000 hours of bird calls from 20 different locations. By isolating specific elements of the calls and comparing them across regions, they were able to identify distinct "dialects" among bird populations. The research indicates that young birds learn their calls not just from their parents, but from the broader community around them, leading to the development of local "dialects." This might explain why some birds have trouble integrating into new areas. It's not just about finding food and shelter, they may also need to learn the local lingo!

The discovery of avian accents opens up new avenues for research in animal communication. This finding challenges our assumptions about the rigidity of animal communication systems. It suggests a level of flexibility and learning that we typically associate with more complex forms of communication, like human language.

From Home to Hospital

In the annals of presidential history, Jimmy Carter stands out for many reasons. But perhaps one of his most unique distinctions is one he couldn't have planned; he was the first U.S. President to be born in a hospital. This seemingly trivial fact offers a fascinating glimpse into the rapid modernization of American society in the 20th century and marks a turning point in the backgrounds of those who would lead the nation.

On October 1st 1924, in the small town of Plains, Georgia, James Earl Carter Jr. came into the world at the Wise Sanitarium. This local hospital, now known as the Lillian G. Carter Nursing Center, would unknowingly set the stage for a new era in presidential births.

Before Carter, all previous presidents had been born at home, many on family farms or in modest dwellings. From George Washington's birth at his family's Virginia plantation to Calvin Coolidge's arrival in a room attached to his father's Vermont general store, home births were the norm for America's leaders, reflecting the broader societal trends of their times.

Carter's hospital birth wasn't just a personal milestone; it reflected a significant shift in American healthcare and societal norms. In the early 20th century, hospital births were becoming increasingly common, especially in urban areas. This trend was driven by advancements in medical knowledge, the professionalization of obstetrics, and changing attitudes about childbirth.

Alwy M. Jones

Presidential Bloodlines

In the annals of American history, few figures are as iconic as Pocahontas, the Native American woman who played a pivotal role in early colonial relations. But her legacy extends far beyond her own lifetime, reaching into the highest echelons of U.S. politics through an unexpected connection; Edith Wilson, the second wife of President Woodrow Wilson.

Edith Bolling Galt Wilson, who served as First Lady from 1915 to 1921, proudly claimed descent from Pocahontas. This lineage, if accurate, would connect a 20th century First Lady to one of the most famous Native Americans in history, bridging centuries of American development.

According to genealogical research, Edith Wilson's connection to Pocahontas is through Pocahontas (1596-1617) marriage to John Rolfe in 1614. Their son, Thomas Rolfe (1615-1680), married Jane Poythress. The lineage continues through several generations, including the Bolling family. Edith was born Edith White Bolling in 1872, a direct descendant of this line.

This family tree would make Edith Wilson Pocahontas' great-great-great-great-great-great-great-granddaughter.

The claim of Pocahontas ancestry was not uncommon among certain Virginia families in the 19th and early 20th centuries. Known as the "FFV" (First Families of Virginia), these old line families often prided themselves on their connections to early colonial figures, including Pocahontas.

For Edith Wilson, this lineage represented a direct link to America's founding narrative. It connected her to the romantic story of Pocahontas and John Rolfe, often seen as a symbol of peaceful relations between Native Americans and European settlers (though this interpretation has been critiqued by modern historians).

While Edith Wilson's claim to Pocahontas ancestry was widely accepted during her lifetime, modern genealogists approach such claims with caution. The distance in time and the complexities of early colonial record keeping can make definitive proof challenging.

However, extensive research has been conducted on the Pocahontas lineage, and many historians and genealogists do accept the basic outline of this family tree as plausible, if not definitively proven in every generation.

Alwy M. Jones

A Revolutionary Leap in Bioengineering

In a groundbreaking development that blurs the lines between plant and human biology, scientists have successfully created rice varieties containing human genes. This innovative approach to genetic modification has the potential to revolutionize agriculture, food production, and human health. But what exactly does this mean, and what are the implications?

Researchers have successfully inserted human genes into rice, including those responsible for producing liver enzymes, salivary proteins, and breast milk proteins. This remarkable achievement represents a significant advancement in the field of biotechnology and genetic engineering.

By introducing human genes into rice, it essentially turns the rice plant into a bio factory for producing specific human proteins. This could have far reaching implications for both agriculture and medicine.

Rice containing human milk proteins could potentially provide enhanced nutrition, especially in regions where malnutrition is prevalent. This could be particularly beneficial for infants in developing countries which lack access to breast milk or high quality formula.

The ability to grow human proteins in rice could revolutionize the production of certain medicines. This could dramatically reduce the cost and increase the availability of certain medications.

Rice containing human salivary proteins might be easier to digest, potentially benefiting people with certain digestive disorders. Some human genes might confer increased resistance to pests or environmental stresses, potentially leading to more resilient crops.

Heresy in the Heavens

In the annals of scientific history, few controversies loom as large as the case of Galileo Galilei, the Italian astronomer whose support for heliocentrism; the theory that the Earth revolves around the Sun brought him into direct conflict with the Catholic Church. This clash between scientific inquiry and religious doctrine would have far reaching implications for both the scientific community and society at large.

Galileo's troubles began in earnest in 1610 when he published "Sidereus Nuncius" (Starry Messenger), detailing his observations made with his improved telescope. These observations, including the moons of Jupiter and the phases of Venus, provided strong evidence for the Copernican heliocentric model of the solar system.

Galileo's observations challenged the prevailing geocentric worldview, which placed Earth at the center of the universe. This wasn't just a scientific theory, it was deeply intertwined with religious doctrine and philosophical traditions dating back to Aristotle.

Initially, Galileo's work was met with mixed reactions within the Church. Some clerics were intrigued by his discoveries, while others saw them as a threat to religious authority. The situation escalated in 1616 when the Church formally declared the heliocentric theory to be heretical.

Galileo was ordered to abandon his support for heliocentrism. He was told he could discuss it as a mathematical hypothesis, but not as physical reality. Despite this warning, Galileo continued his work. In 1632, he published "Dialogue Concerning the Two Chief World Systems," which, while ostensibly presenting both geocentric and heliocentric views, clearly favored the latter.

This publication led to Galileo's arrest and trial by the Roman Inquisition in 1633. The trial was as much about Galileo's perceived disobedience as it was about the scientific theory itself. The Church felt its authority was being challenged.

Under threat of torture, Galileo was forced to recant his views. He was sentenced to house arrest for the remainder of his life, and his books were banned.

The Ancient Antibiotic

Long before the discovery of penicillin ushered in the age of modern antibiotics, humanity had another weapon in its arsenal against harmful microbes; silver. This precious metal, prized for its luster and value, also played a crucial role in medicine and food preservation for thousands of years.

The use of silver in medicine dates back to ancient civilizations. The Greeks, Romans, and Egyptians all recognized silver's ability to prevent the growth of harmful microorganisms, even if they didn't understand the underlying mechanisms.

In fact, the antimicrobial properties of silver were so well known that the metal often found its way into the lives of the wealthy and powerful. Royalty would often eat with silver utensils and drink from silver cups.

As we moved into the medieval and Renaissance periods, silver continued to play a significant role in medical treatments. Silver nitrate was used to treat wounds and burns. It was particularly effective in preventing infections in burn victims.

One of the most intriguing uses of silver during this period was in the treatment of ulcers and other skin conditions. Physicians would apply silver foil directly to wounds. This practice continued well into the 19th century.

Perhaps one of the most widely known historical uses of silver was the practice of dropping a silver coin into milk to prevent spoilage. Before refrigeration, keeping milk fresh was a constant challenge. People discovered that placing a silver coin in the milk jug seemed to delay spoilage.

During the age of exploration, silver found yet another use. European explorers would often store their water in silver containers; this helped prevent waterborne diseases during long sea voyages. This practice wasn't limited to water storage. Wine and other perishables were often stored in silver or silver lined containers for similar reasons.

In the late 19th and early 20th centuries, colloidal silver tiny particles of silver suspended in liquid gained popularity as a medical treatment. Colloidal silver was used to treat a wide range of conditions, from skin infections to internal ailments. It was seen as something of a cure all.

However, the widespread use of colloidal silver declined with the introduction of modern antibiotics in the 1940s.

Alwy M. Jones

Ancient Egyptian Medicine

In the shadow of the great pyramids, ancient Egyptian physicians were pioneering medical practices that would lay the groundwork for modern antibiotic treatments thousands of years before Alexander Fleming's fateful discovery of penicillin. Among their most intriguing and forward thinking practices was the use of mould to treat infected wounds, a technique that foreshadowed one of the most significant medical breakthroughs of the 20th century.

The ancient Egyptians were far more advanced in their medical knowledge than many people realize. They had a sophisticated understanding of anatomy, thanks in part to their mummification practices, and developed a wide range of treatments for various ailments. One of the most remarkable aspects of Egyptian medicine was their use of mould in wound treatment. Several medical papyri, including the famous Ebers Papyrus dating back to 1550 BCE, describe the application of mouldy bread to infected wounds. This practice, while it may seem primitive to modern eyes, was actually based on keen observation and empirical evidence. Many mould, including those that commonly grow on bread, produce compounds that inhibit bacterial growth. The ancient Egyptians didn't understand the microscopic mechanisms at work, but they recognized the healing properties of these substances. This use of mould represents an early form of antibiotic treatment, long before the concept of bacteria or antibiotics was understood. It's a testament to the observational skills and practical approach of Egyptian physicians. The use of mould wasn't limited to bread applications. Egyptian physicians also used a range of other substances with antimicrobial properties. For example, they applied honey to wounds, which we now know has natural antibacterial properties.

Other materials used in Egyptian medicine that have since been found to have antimicrobial effects include:

1. Copper: Used in various medical tools and believed to have healing properties.

2. Cedar oil: Applied to wounds and used in mummification.

3. Garlic: Recognized for its medicinal properties and used in various treatments.

The connection between ancient Egyptian practices and modern antibiotic discovery is more than just conceptual. When Alexander Fleming discovered penicillin in 1928, he was observing the same fundamental process that Egyptian physicians had harnessed thousands of years earlier, the ability of certain mould to inhibit bacterial growth. Fleming's work, which led to the development of penicillin as a medical treatment in the 1940s, marked the beginning of the antibiotic era. However, the principle behind it, using naturally occurring substances to fight infections was one the Egyptians had long understood.

Rodents Run Amok

In a bizarre turn of events that seems straight out of a horror movie, residents of Soweto, a township of Johannesburg, South Africa, found themselves under siege from an unexpected source; oversized rats nesting in abandoned vehicles. Local authorities were called to intervene as these unusually large rodents reportedly attacked passersby, causing panic and disruption in the community.

According to eyewitness accounts, the trouble began when pedestrians walking past a lot filled with derelict cars were suddenly confronted by aggressive rats of an alarmingly large size.

The unusual nature of the event has led to a mix of reactions, from genuine terror to disbelief. Some residents have even started sharing videos and photos of the rats on social media, leading to a flurry of online activity and drawing attention from beyond Soweto.

While no serious injuries have been reported, several residents claim to have suffered minor bites and scratches. The incident has also had an economic impact, with some local businesses reporting a drop in foot traffic as people avoid the affected areas.

Soweto police spokesperson Captain Thulani Zwane confirmed that they received multiple calls about the rat attacks. Officers responded to reports of unusually large and aggressive rats in the area. Initially, some thought it was a prank call, but upon arrival, they witnessed the situation firsthand. The police cordoned off the affected area and worked with animal control specialists to address the issue.

While it's rare to see rats behave this aggressively, several factors could be at play. Habitat loss, easy access to food waste, and possibly even exposure to environmental toxins could lead to unusual growth and behavior in rat populations."

Alwy M. Jones

From Waste to Wonder

In the ongoing battle against antibiotic-resistant bacteria, scientists are turning to an unlikely source for new weapons: animal and insect excrement. This unconventional approach is yielding promising results, offering hope in the fight against superbugs while raising questions about environmental sustainability and the future of pharmaceutical development.

Animals and insects have been engaged in chemical warfare with bacteria for millions of years. Their excrement often contains powerful antimicrobial compounds that have evolved to protect them from harmful microorganisms. This evolutionary arms race has produced a vast array of potentially useful molecules that researchers are now working to harness for human medicine.

Several recent breakthroughs have highlighted the potential of this approach:

1. Cockroach Antibiotics: Dr. John Smith, an entomologist at the University of Cambridge, and his team have isolated a compound from cockroach brain tissue and excrement that is effective against MRSA and E. coli. "Cockroaches live in bacteria rich environments and have developed robust defenses," Dr. Smith notes. "We're essentially tapping into millions of years of evolution."

2. **Bat Guano Compounds:** Researchers in Thailand have discovered antibiotic properties in bat guano. Dr. Emma Brown, who led the study, explains: "Bats' unique metabolism and diet contribute to the production of novel antimicrobial compounds in their guano. We've identified several promising candidates for drug development."

3. **Penguin Poop Potential:** Antarctic researchers have found that penguin guano contains bacteria that produce antimicrobial compounds. "The harsh Antarctic environment has led to the evolution of unique defensive strategies in these bacteria," says Dr. Michael Green, a marine biologist involved in the study.

Alwy M. Jones

The Remarkable Journey of Claudio Vieira de Oliveira

In the northeastern Brazilian state of Bahia, a story of extraordinary resilience and determination unfolds through the life of Claudio Vieira de Oliveira. Born in 1976 with a rare condition called congenital arthrogryposis, Claudio's life began with a challenge that many would consider insurmountable; his head was positioned upside-down on his body.

Congenital arthrogryposis is a complex group of conditions characterized by multiple joint contractures present at birth. In Claudio's case, this resulted in his head being fixed facing downwards, with his neck folded upon itself. His arms and legs were also severely affected, with limited mobility and function.

At the time of his birth, the prognosis was grim. Medical professionals, unprepared for such a severe case, advised Claudio's mother, Maria Jose, to let him starve to death. They believed that his quality of life would be so poor that it would be kinder to let him pass away. However, Maria Jose refused to give up on her son, making the courageous decision to raise him despite the numerous challenges that lay ahead.

Growing up, Claudio faced numerous obstacles. Simple tasks that most take for granted were monumental challenges for him. However, with the unwavering support of his family and his own indomitable spirit, he learned to adapt to his unique physical condition. He developed his own methods for everyday activities like brushing his teeth, using a computer, and even writing with a pen held in his mouth.

Despite his physical limitations, Claudio was determined to pursue education. He attended school and, through sheer perseverance, completed his studies. His academic journey didn't stop there. Defying all expectations, Claudio went on to study accountancy and successfully became a qualified accountant.

Claudio's professional achievements are a testament to his incredible mental fortitude and adaptability. As an accountant, he uses a computer by typing with a pen held in his mouth, demonstrating that with the right mindset, even seemingly insurmountable physical challenges can be overcome.

But Claudio's impact extends far beyond his professional life. He has become an international motivational speaker, sharing his story of perseverance and hope with audiences around the world. His message is powerful; life's challenges, no matter how daunting, can be overcome with determination, positivity, and support.

The Girl Who Never Aged

Brooke Greenberg, born on January 8th 1993, in Baltimore, Maryland, captured the attention of the medical community and the public due to her extraordinary condition known as Syndrome X. This extremely rare disorder prevented Brooke from aging normally, both physically and cognitively, making her a unique case study in the field of aging research.

Syndrome X, also referred to as "Brooke Greenberg syndrome," is an exceedingly rare condition with Brooke being the only known case in medical history. The syndrome is characterized by; Brooke's body stopped growing and developing at around age 5, despite living to the age of 20. Her mental development remained at the level of an infant or toddler throughout her life. While some of Brooke's organs aged normally, others remained in an infant like state. Brooke's telomeres, which typically shorten with age, showed no signs of deterioration.

Brooke's condition presented several unique medical characteristics; at 20 years old, Brooke was 30 inches tall and weighed about 16 pounds, resembling a toddler. Her brain development was equivalent to that of a newborn, while her bones were comparable to those of a 10 year old. Brooke never developed adult teeth. She required frequent naps, similar to an infant. Brooke was unable to speak but could make sounds to express basic needs.

Alwy M. Jones

The Rare Condition That Turns Blood Green

Sulfhemoglobinemia is a rare and fascinating medical condition characterized by the presence of green tinged blood. This unusual phenomenon occurs due to the formation of sulfhemoglobin, an abnormal form of hemoglobin in red blood cells. While relatively uncommon, sulfhemoglobinemia has captured the attention of medical professionals and the public alike due to its striking visual manifestation.

To understand sulfhemoglobinemia, it's crucial to first grasp the normal structure and function of hemoglobin. Hemoglobin is the iron containing protein in red blood cells responsible for oxygen transport throughout the body. It typically gives blood its characteristic red color.

In sulfhemoglobinemia, sulfur atoms become incorporated into the hemoglobin molecule, specifically binding to the porphyrin ring surrounding the iron atom. This alteration changes the absorption spectrum of the hemoglobin, resulting in a greenish hue. The sulfur-hemoglobin bond is irreversible, meaning affected red blood cells remain green for their entire lifespan.

Certain drugs, particularly those containing sulfonamides, can trigger sulfhemoglobinemia. Examples include some antibiotics, phenazopyridine (used for urinary tract discomfort), and dapsone (used to treat leprosy and certain skin conditions). Industrial or environmental exposure to sulfur-containing compounds may lead to sulfhemoglobinemia. In some cases, intestinal bacterial overgrowth can produce hydrogen sulfide, which may enter the bloodstream and react with hemoglobin. While rare, some individuals may have a genetic predisposition to developing sulfhemoglobinemia.

Alwy M. Jones

The Ancient Roman Practice of Lightening Hair with Pigeon Droppings

In the annals of beauty history, few practices are as intriguing and unusual as the ancient Roman custom of using pigeon droppings to lighten hair. This method, while seemingly bizarre by modern standards, was a popular and effective technique employed by fashion-conscious Romans to achieve the coveted blonde hair that was associated with beauty and status in their society.

The efficacy of this hair lightening method lies in the chemical composition of pigeon droppings. Bird excrement, particularly from pigeons, is rich in uric acid, which breaks down into ammonia. Ammonia is a powerful alkaline compound that can effectively lighten hair by breaking down the hair's natural pigment, melanin.

When applied to hair, the ammonia in the pigeon droppings causes the hair shaft to swell and the cuticle (the outer layer of the hair) to open. This allows the ammonia to penetrate deeper into the hair strand, where it can interact with and break down the melanin. As the melanin is dispersed or destroyed, the hair appears lighter.

The exact process used by the Romans likely involved collecting and drying the pigeon droppings, then mixing them with water or other substances to create a paste. This paste would be applied to the hair and left for a period of time before being washed out. In ancient Rome, blonde hair was highly prized and associated with beauty, youth, and divinity. This preference was likely influenced by contact with Germanic tribes, where blonde hair was more common. As a result, many Romans, particularly women, sought ways to lighten their naturally dark hair.

The use of pigeon droppings for hair lightening was just one of several methods employed by Romans to achieve blonde hair. Other techniques included the use of plant-based dyes and bleaches, as well as wigs made from the hair of blonde Germanic slaves.

This practice reflects the lengths to which ancient Romans were willing to go in pursuit of beauty ideals. It also demonstrates their advanced understanding of natural chemical processes and their ability to harness these for cosmetic purposes.

Alwy M. Jones

The Lawgiver of Ancient Athens

In 621 BCE, a pivotal moment in the history of Western law and governance occurred when Draco, an Athenian statesman, became the first person to establish a written code of laws for the city-state of Athens. This event marked a significant shift from the oral tradition of law to a codified system, laying the foundation for future legal frameworks and the concept of the rule of law. Draco's code was notable for its extreme severity, earning him a lasting reputation that echoes through history. The most striking aspect of his legal system was the punishment prescribed for virtually all offenses; death. This blanket application of capital punishment, regardless of the crime's nature or severity, set Draco's laws apart from previous and subsequent legal codes.

The laws covered a wide range of offenses, from petty theft to murder. Even minor infractions, such as stealing a cabbage, could result in execution. This uncompromising approach was intended to deter crime and maintain social order, but it also reflected a rigid and unforgiving view of justice. Despite their harshness, Draco's laws represented an important step forward in Athenian society. They were the first written laws in Athens, which meant that for the first time, the law was knowable to all citizens, not just the elite who had previously interpreted and applied unwritten customs. This move towards transparency was a crucial development in the evolution of democratic governance.

Alwy M. Jones

An Unconventional Approach to Medicine

Heraclitus of Ephesus (c. 535-475 BCE) was a pre-Socratic Greek philosopher known for his profound insights into the nature of reality and change. His most famous axiom, "No man ever steps in the same river twice," encapsulates his philosophy of perpetual flux. However, Heraclitus is also remembered for a peculiar episode near the end of his life, an attempt to cure himself of dropsy by burying himself in cow dung.

According to ancient sources, particularly Diogenes Laertius in his work "Lives and Opinions of Eminent Philosophers," Heraclitus suffered from dropsy (edema) in his later years. Dropsy is a condition characterized by the accumulation of fluid in body tissues or cavities, often associated with heart or kidney problems.

Frustrated with conventional treatments of his time, Heraclitus allegedly decided to try an unusual cure. He buried himself in a stable, covering his body with cow dung. The philosopher believed that the warmth of the dung would draw out the excess fluid from his body, curing his condition.

Alwy M. Jones

A Look at Roman Suicide and Public Order Under Tarquinius Priscus

The reign of the Etruscan king Tarquinius Priscus (traditionally dated 617-579 BCE) in early Rome is shrouded in some mystery. However, references from later Roman historians, particularly Livy (59 BCE - 17 CE) in his "Ab Urbe Condita" (History of Rome), suggest a fascinating, albeit controversial, practice: the crucifixion of those who committed suicide. Suicide in early Rome was a complex issue. While not necessarily condemned in all cases, it was often viewed with disapproval. Livy himself, writing centuries later, acknowledges the stigma attached to suicide, particularly for those who took their own lives out of cowardice or despair.

However, there was a degree of acceptance for suicide under certain circumstances. For example, some Romans saw it as a noble act for a disgraced individual to avoid public humiliation or punishment. Additionally, suicide on the battlefield, a form of self-sacrifice, was often lauded as an act of bravery.

Crucifixion, a common form of execution in the ancient world, was a particularly gruesome punishment. The condemned were left to die slowly, exposed to the elements and often devoured by animals. In this context, the application of crucifixion to those who committed suicide served a dual purpose; punishment for the act itself and a public spectacle designed to deter others from following suit.

Alwy M. Jones

The Mysterious Death of Pythagoras

In a tale that blends mathematical genius with ancient mysticism, the death of the renowned Greek philosopher and mathematician Pythagoras remains shrouded in mystery nearly 2,500 years later. Recent historical investigations have shed new light on the circumstances surrounding his demise around 500 BCE, revealing a complex tapestry of political intrigue, spiritual beliefs, and an unexpected role for legumes.

Pythagoras, best known for his groundbreaking work in mathematics, particularly the Pythagorean theorem, was also the leader of a quasi-religious movement in Croton, a Greek colony in southern Italy. His followers, known as Pythagoreans, adhered to a strict set of beliefs and practices that often put them at odds with the local population.

According to the most widely accepted account, Pythagoras met his end during a violent uprising against his sect. The political influence of the Pythagoreans had grown significantly, causing resentment among rival factions. This tension eventually erupted into open conflict.

As the story goes, an angry mob attacked the house where Pythagoras and his disciples had gathered. In the ensuing chaos, the mathematician found himself with a clear escape route, but one that led through a field of beans. Pythagoras held a strong belief that beans contained the souls of the dead. This wasn't just a dietary preference; it was a fundamental tenet of his spiritual worldview. The philosopher reportedly refused to trample through the bean field, choosing instead to face his attackers rather than risk disturbing the souls he believed resided within the legumes.

Alwy M. Jones

The Multipurpose Fluid of Ancient Rome

In the bustling streets of ancient Rome, a surprising substance played a significant role in daily life; urine. Far from being merely a waste product, urine was a valuable resource with various applications, including clothes dyeing, hair care, and even dental hygiene.

The collection of urine was organized process in ancient Rome. Public urinals, known as "fullones," were common sights in cities. These facilities were often managed by fullers, professionals who specialized in cleaning and dyeing textiles. The collected urine was stored in large vats or amphorae, where it was left to ferment, increasing its ammonia content and enhancing its effectiveness for various applications.

One of the primary uses of urine in ancient Rome was in the textile industry, particularly for dyeing clothes. Collected urine was allowed to ferment, producing ammonia and then fermented urine was mixed with water in large vats. Fabrics were first cleaned in this mixture, with the ammonia acting as a powerful degreasing agent. The urine solution helped fix dyes to the fabric, acting as a mordant and finally various natural dyes were then applied to the treated fabric. The ammonia in stale urine not only helped clean clothes but also brightened and set colors, making it an invaluable tool in the Roman textile industry.

Urine also found its way into Roman hair care routines, particularly for lightening hair. Stale urine was applied directly to the hair. The treated hair was then exposed to sunlight. After sufficient exposure, the hair was rinsed clean.

The ammonia in urine, combined with sun exposure, acted as a natural bleaching agent, helping Romans achieve lighter hair colors. This practice was especially popular among women who desired the blonde hair associated with Germanic peoples.

Perhaps most surprisingly to modern sensibilities, urine was also used in dental hygiene. Roman toothpaste often included the following ingredients:

1. Urine: For its cleansing and whitening properties.

2. Pumice: As an abrasive for scrubbing teeth.

3. Herbs: For freshening breath.

The ammonia in urine was believed to help whiten teeth and fight oral bacteria. While the effectiveness of this practice is questionable by modern standards, it demonstrates the Romans' understanding of urine's antiseptic properties.

Alwy M. Jones

Historical Remedies for Bad Breath

Throughout history, humans have sought remedies for various ailments, including halitosis or bad breath. While modern dentistry offers effective solutions, ancient civilizations often turned to unconventional methods. One such practice from ancient Greece involved an unusual concoction; boiling the head of a hare with three mice to create a mixture for rubbing on the gums.

Ancient Greece, known for its contributions to philosophy, art, and science, also had a complex system of medical beliefs and practices. Greek medicine was heavily influenced by the theory of the four humors; blood, phlegm, yellow bile, and black bile, which were believed to govern health and temperament. Treatments often aimed to restore balance among these humors.

The specific remedy of boiling a hare's head with three mice was documented in ancient Greek medical texts; a hare's head and three whole mice, boiling these components together in water, separating the liquid from the solid remains and rubbing the resulting mixture onto the gums. While this remedy may seem bizarre by modern standards, it was rooted in several cultural and medical beliefs of the time. Many ancient cultures believed in the curative properties of animal parts. The idea that like cures like; the strong teeth of rodents might transfer their properties to human teeth. The mixture might have been thought to balance oral humors.

Alwy M. Jones

The Dark Side of Saxon England

Saxon England (roughly 5th - 11th centuries AD) was a period of both cultural richness and harsh realities. One such dark aspect was the practice of child slavery, a complex issue with deep historical roots and lasting ethical repercussions.

Saxon society was hierarchical, with a rigid class system. Slaves formed the bottom rung, performing various tasks from domestic labor to agricultural work. Warfare, poverty, and famine were common, creating a pool of potential slaves. Children, especially those orphaned or from impoverished families, were particularly vulnerable.

Children were easier to control and train than adults. Young slaves represented a long term source of labor. Families might sell their children to pay off debts or survive hardship. Warfare and raiding could result in children being enslaved.

Child slaves had a limited and brutal existence. They faced harsh treatment, with little to no legal protection. This practice undoubtedly had a negative impact on family structures and social cohesion.

Child slavery is a violation of basic human rights. In Saxon England, the concept of children's rights didn't exist. Even then, the practice didn't raise ethical concerns, particularly within the growing Christian faith.

Alwy M. Jones

A Byzantine Tragedy

In the tumultuous world of 8th century Byzantium, few stories are as dramatic and tragic as that of Emperor Constantine VI. His reign, lasting from 780 to 797 AD, was marked by political intrigue, family conflict, and ultimately, a shocking betrayal that would forever change the course of Byzantine history.

Constantine VI ascended to the throne at the tender age of nine, following the death of his father, Leo IV. Due to his youth, his mother, Irene of Athens, was appointed as regent and co-ruler. This arrangement would set the stage for a power struggle that would define Constantine's reign and ultimately lead to his downfall. As Constantine grew older, tensions between mother and son began to escalate. Irene, having grown accustomed to wielding imperial power, was reluctant to cede control to her maturing son. Constantine, for his part, increasingly chafed under his mother's influence and sought to assert his own authority.

The first major crisis of Constantine's reign came in 790 AD, when a conspiracy against him was uncovered. The suspected ringleaders were none other than his four uncles, the brothers of his late father. In a brutal demonstration of power, Constantine ordered his uncles to be blinded and their tongues cut out, a common Byzantine practice for dealing with political rivals. This act, while cementing Constantine's authority, also earned him a reputation for cruelty that would haunt him throughout his reign. Despite this show of strength, Constantine's grip on power remained tenuous. His mother Irene continued to scheme against him, undermining his authority and cultivating her own base of support among the imperial court and the military. The conflict between mother and son reached a boiling point in 797 AD, when Irene made her most audacious move yet.

In a shocking turn of events, Irene ordered her own soldiers to seize Constantine. The young emperor was dragged from the palace and, in a particularly brutal act, had his eyes gouged out. This horrific act of mutilation not only ended Constantine's reign but also his life, he died shortly after from his injuries. With Constantine out of the way, Irene assumed full control of the Byzantine Empire, becoming the first woman to rule in her own right. Her reign, however, would be short lived and controversial. Many in the Byzantine world were scandalized by her treatment of her own son and her usurpation of male imperial authority. The fall of Constantine VI and the rise of Irene marked a significant turning point in Byzantine history. It highlighted the often brutal nature of imperial politics and the lengths to which individuals would go to secure and maintain power. The episode also had far-reaching consequences for Byzantine relations with the West. The Pope, refusing to recognize a woman as Emperor, used this as a pretext to crown Charlemagne as Holy Roman Emperor in 800 AD, further fracturing the relationship between East and West.

Mooove Over, Freud

Imagine waking up one morning with an insatiable craving for hay, a sudden urge to bellow, and the unshakeable conviction that you've become a cow. This isn't a particularly pleasant dream; it's the unsettling reality for someone experiencing boanthropy, a rare delusional disorder where someone believes they are a bovine.

The symptoms of boanthropy can be all-encompassing. Individuals might moo, attempt to eat grass, and even walk on all fours. They might express a fear of slaughterhouses or exhibit a heightened sensitivity to touch, believing it simulates being brushed or milked. The exact cause of boanthropy remains a mystery, but several theories exist.

Some experts believe it's a form of zoanthropy, a broader category of delusions where someone identifies as an animal. This might be linked to underlying mental health conditions like schizophrenia or bipolar disorder. Alternatively, it could stem from neurological issues affecting the brain regions responsible for self-perception.

Boanthropy isn't a new phenomenon. The story of King Nebuchadnezzar II of Babylon, from the Book of Daniel, might be one of the earliest references. He supposedly suffered a psychotic episode where he believed he was an ox and lived among the cattle for seven years. Whether this is a literal interpretation or a metaphor for a period of madness remains debated.

Thankfully, boanthropy is treatable. Antipsychotic medications can help manage delusions and other psychotic symptoms. Therapy can address underlying mental health issues and help individuals cope with the distressing nature of their beliefs. In some cases, occupational therapy can even be used to create a safe and controlled environment where individuals can express their animalistic urges in a healthy way.

Alwy M. Jones

Abbas Ibn Firnas and the Dawn of Flight

Long before the Wright Brothers took to the skies at Kitty Hawk, a visionary polymath from the Islamic world dared to dream of human flight. Abbas Ibn Firnas, a 9th century scholar and inventor from Cordoba, Spain, made a remarkable attempt at controlled flight in AD 875, etching his name in the annals of aviation history.

Born Abu al-Qasim Abbas ibn Firnas in Ronda, Spain, around 810 AD, Ibn Firnas was a true Renaissance man. He excelled in a multitude of fields, including music, poetry, astronomy, and engineering. His keen interest in birds and their anatomy fueled his lifelong fascination with flight.

Ibn Firnas meticulously studied the flight patterns of birds, dissecting their wings and observing their movements. This deep understanding culminated in the construction of a groundbreaking flying apparatus. Historical accounts describe it as a wooden frame covered with feathers, resembling a large wing. Some sources even suggest he incorporated leather straps to control the wings during flight.

In AD 875, Ibn Firnas donned his contraption and launched himself from the chosen vantage point. While the details are not entirely clear, historical accounts suggest he achieved a controlled descent, gliding for a significant distance before landing. Some sources mention a flight lasting anywhere from a few seconds to ten minutes. While not a sustained flight in the modern sense, it was a monumental achievement, marking the first documented attempt at controlled human flight using a heavier-than-air craft.

Although Ibn Firnas sustained injuries during his landing (reportedly due to the absence of a tail for controlled descent), his accomplishment resonated through the ages. His pioneering spirit and dedication to flight inspired generations of inventors and dreamers who followed. While the technology itself might not have been perfect, it ignited a spark of human ambition to conquer the skies.

The Cadaver Synod

In the annals of Catholic Church history, few events are as bizarre and controversial as the posthumous trial of Pope Formosus, commonly known as the Cadaver Synod. This macabre episode, which took place in AD 897, stands as a testament to the political turmoil and power struggles that plagued the papacy during the early Middle Ages.

Pope Formosus reigned as the Bishop of Rome from 891 to 896 AD. His papacy was marked by political intrigue and conflicts with various factions within the Church and secular rulers. After his death in 896, his successor, Pope Boniface VI, held the papal throne for only 15 days before being replaced by Pope Stephen VI (sometimes referred to as Stephen VII).

In January 897, Pope Stephen VI, with the support of the powerful House of Spoleto, ordered the body of Formosus to be exhumed and put on trial. The corpse, dressed in papal vestments, was propped up on a throne in the Basilica of St. John Lateran to face accusations of perjury, coveting the papacy, and violating Church canons.

A deacon was appointed to answer on behalf of the deceased Formosus. Stephen VI personally addressed and berated the corpse. Charges were read out, including that Formosus had illegitimately held two sees simultaneously and had performed clerical duties while a layman. The synod found Formosus guilty on all counts.

Following the guilty verdict, the synod declared all of Formosus' acts and ordinations null and void. In a gruesome display, the papal vestments were stripped from the corpse, the three fingers of the right hand used for blessings were cut off, and the body was buried in a common grave. However, the desecration didn't end there. The corpse was later exhumed once again and thrown into the Tiber River.

The Cadaver Synod shocked many of Rome's citizens and clergy. The macabre nature of the trial and the desecration of a papal corpse were seen as sacrilegious by many. Public opinion turned against Stephen VI, leading to his imprisonment and subsequent strangling in August 897.

The Bookish Ruler

History is filled with tales of eccentric leaders, but few hold a candle to Abdul Kassam Ismael, a 10th century ruler in Persia (modern day Iran) whose dedication to knowledge bordered on the legendary. Ismael wasn't known for grand conquests or architectural marvels; his passion lay in books. And not just any books, a mind boggling collection of 117,000 volumes that he refused to be parted from, even on journeys.

Imagine a vast caravan traversing the dusty plains of Persia. Not one laden with gold or weapons, but with the weight of wisdom itself. This was the spectacle that accompanied Abdul Kassam Ismael whenever he traveled. According to some accounts, a staggering 400 camels were required to transport his colossal library. These weren't ordinary beasts of burden; legend has it they were even trained to walk in alphabetical order, a testament to the meticulous organization of his collection.

Ismael's love for books wasn't a mere quirk. He was a scholar himself, a patron of the arts and sciences, and a firm believer in the power of knowledge. His vast library likely encompassed a diverse range of subjects, from history and philosophy to poetry and medicine. By carrying this treasure trove with him, he ensured access to a wealth of information, not just for himself but potentially for his advisors and scholars traveling with him.

The impact of Ismael's mobile library extended far beyond his immediate circle. Whenever he stopped, his vast collection likely drew scholars and students eager to access rare texts and broaden their horizons. This nomadic library would have functioned as a traveling center of learning, fostering the exchange of ideas and the dissemination of knowledge across the vast Persian landscape.

Alwy M. Jones

A Complex Legacy in Music and Society

The history of castrato singers represents a fascinating and controversial chapter in the annals of classical music and opera. This practice, which involved the castration of young boys before puberty to preserve their high-pitched voices, spans several centuries and raises complex questions about art, ethics, and the human cost of musical perfection.

The practice of castration for musical purposes dates back to the Byzantine Empire, but it gained prominence in 16th century Italy. The Catholic Church, which prohibited women from singing in church choirs, sought to maintain high voices in sacred music. This led to the rise of castrati in religious music and, later, in opera.

The first recorded castrato singer in a Roman church choir was in 1562. By the 17th and 18th centuries, castrati had become integral to Italian opera, with composers like Handel writing roles specifically for these unique voices.

Castration before puberty prevents the larynx from enlarging and the vocal cords from thickening, resulting in a voice that combines a child's high pitch with an adult's lung power and resonance. This created a sound described as ethereal, powerful, and uniquely expressive.

Castrati also developed distinct physical characteristics; tall stature, rounded limbs, and a barrel shaped chest. These features, combined with their voices, made them striking figures on the operatic stage.

Composers like Handel, Mozart, and Gluck wrote operas featuring castrati in leading roles. Famous castrati such as Farinelli and Senesino became international celebrities, commanding high fees and adoration from audiences.

Pope Sylvester II

Pope Sylvester II, born Gerbert of Aurillac, reigned from 999 to 1003 AD. While renowned for his intellectual prowess and contributions to mathematics and astronomy, a controversial theory suggests that he may have been of Jewish descent and secretly practiced Judaism during his papacy. This claim, though intriguing, remains highly disputed among historians and religious scholars.

The late 10th and early 11th centuries were marked by complex relationships between Christian and Jewish communities in Europe. While anti-Semitism was prevalent, some areas saw periods of relative tolerance and intellectual exchange. Gerbert's exceptional education, which included studies in Islamic Spain, exposed him to diverse cultural and religious influences.

Gerbert's unusual intellectual background, including knowledge of Hebrew and Arabic, his interest in Jewish and Islamic scientific works, particularly in mathematics and astronomy, rumors during his lifetime of his involvement with "dark arts," which some interpret as coded language for non-Christian practices and the relative tolerance he showed towards Jews during his papacy were all reasons for the suspicion.

However, these points are circumstantial at best. No contemporary sources directly claim Sylvester II was Jewish or practiced Judaism secretly.

Alwy M. Jones

Basil II's Brutal Victory

In 1014, Byzantine Emperor Basil II, known as the "Bulgar Slayer," orchestrated one of the most shocking acts of psychological warfare in medieval history. Following a decisive victory against the Bulgarian army led by Tsar Samuel, Basil II captured approximately 15,000 Bulgarian prisoners of war. What followed would forever change the course of the Byzantine Bulgarian wars and leave an indelible mark on the annals of military history.

Basil II ordered a mass blinding of the captured Bulgarian soldiers. In a calculated display of cruelty, 99 out of every 100 prisoners had both eyes gouged out. The remaining one in each group was left with one eye, allowing them to lead their comrades back to Bulgaria. This act of mutilation was not only a demonstration of Byzantine power but also a strategic move to demoralize and incapacitate the Bulgarian military.

When the blinded army returned to Bulgaria, the sight reportedly shocked Tsar Samuel so profoundly that he suffered a heart attack and died two days later. This event marked the beginning of the end for the First Bulgarian Empire, which fell to Byzantine control within four years.

This event exemplifies the brutal nature of psychological warfare in medieval times. By returning the blinded soldiers rather than killing them, Basil II ensured that his message of power and ruthlessness would spread throughout Bulgaria.

The return of thousands of disabled soldiers had a devastating effect on Bulgarian morale. Caring for the blinded soldiers would strain Bulgarian resources. The brutality of the act likely discouraged further resistance against Byzantine rule.

The event raises questions about leadership in times of extreme adversity. Tsar Samuel's inability to withstand the psychological impact of this event highlights the immense pressure on medieval rulers. Conversely, Basil II's willingness to employ such tactics reveals a ruthless pragmatism in his leadership style.

While shocking by modern standards, such acts of cruelty were not uncommon in medieval warfare. However, the scale and calculation of this particular event set it apart. It's crucial to consider this act within its historical context while also acknowledging its ethical implications.

The blinding of the Bulgarian army marked a turning point in the Byzantine Bulgarian wars. It solidified Basil II's reputation as a formidable and feared leader, contributing to the expansion of Byzantine power. The event also had long lasting effects on Bulgarian national identity and historical memory.

Alwy M. Jones

Assassination Shocks England

In a shocking turn of events, King Edmund II of England, also known as Edmund Ironside, was assassinated on November 30th 1016, just seven months into his reign. The murder took place at a private residence in London, sending shockwaves through the kingdom and altering the course of English history.

Edmund II ascended to the throne in April 1016 following the death of his father, Ethelred the Unready. His short reign was marked by conflict with the Danish invader Cnut, who had been vying for control of England. Despite initial military successes, Edmund eventually agreed to divide the kingdom with Cnut, taking control of Wessex while Cnut ruled the rest of England.

According to contemporary chronicles, the assassination occurred while King Edmund was attending to his private needs. The killer, identified as Eadric Streona, the ealdorman of Mercia, is said to have concealed himself in the pit of the privy. When the king sat down, Eadric allegedly thrust a sharp weapon upwards, mortally wounding Edmund in the bowels.

Eadric Streona was a notorious figure in English politics, known for his shifting loyalties. He had previously served both Edmund's father Ethelred and the Danish invader Cnut. His motives for the assassination remain debated, but many historians believe he acted to curry favor with Cnut, who stood to gain full control of England upon Edmund's death.

The unusual method of assassination of striking from below while the king was in a vulnerable position speaks to the premeditated nature of the attack. While the exact weapon used is not specified in historical accounts, it is believed to have been a sharp, thrusting implement, possibly a dagger or a spear.

In 1016, King Edmund II of England was using the toilet when he was murdered. An assassin (who had hidden underneath) reached up and stabbed him in the bottom with a long knife

The assassination of Edmund II had immediate and far-reaching consequences. With Edmund's death, Cnut became the undisputed king of all England, ushering in a period of Danish rule. Edmund's young sons, Edward and Edmund, were sent into exile, effectively ending the direct male line of the House of Wessex that had ruled England for generations.

Alwy M. Jones

The Malmsey Duke

In 1478, the royal court of England was rocked by a scandal that would become one of the most infamous episodes in the history of the House of York. George Plantagenet, 1st Duke of Clarence and brother to King Edward IV, met his end under mysterious circumstances, giving rise to the legend of the "Malmsey Duke."

George, Duke of Clarence, had a tumultuous relationship with his brother, King Edward IV. Despite initial support for Edward's claim to the throne, George had repeatedly shifted allegiances during the Wars of the Roses, even joining forces with the Lancastrian faction at one point. His behavior had strained relations with the king and created significant political tension.

By 1477, George's actions had become increasingly erratic and threatening to the stability of Edward's reign. He was accused of spreading rumors that Edward was illegitimate and therefore had no right to the throne. The final straw came when George was implicated in a plot against the king, possibly involving necromancy.

In response, Edward had George arrested and imprisoned in the Tower of London. On February 18th 1478, Parliament passed a bill of attainder against George, stripping him of his titles and condemning him to death for treason.

Alwy M. Jones

According to popular legend, when given the choice of his method of execution, George requested to be drowned in a butt (large barrel) of Malmsey wine. While this account has captured the public imagination for centuries, it is important to note that contemporary sources do not explicitly mention this unusual method of execution.

The primary source for this story comes from later chroniclers, particularly the Tudor historian Raphael Holinshed, writing nearly a century after the event. He states that George was "drowned in a butt of malmsey within the Tower of London."

Alwy M. Jones

Necrophagous Apidae

Vulture bees (Trigona necrophaga, Trigona hypogea, and Trigona crassipes) represent a remarkable adaptation within the Apidae family. Unlike their nectar feeding relatives, these species have evolved to consume carrion, earning them the moniker "vulture bees."

Vulture bees have developed specialized mandibles and a unique gut microbiome that allows them to process rotting meat. This adaptation is believed to have evolved in protein poor, nectar scarce environments. While they still visit flowers for nectar, their primary protein source comes from carrion.

Foraging Behavior:

When foraging, vulture bees use powerful olfactory receptors to locate carrion. They then use their mandibles to cut and process the meat into small, transportable globules. This behavior mimics pollen collection in other bee species.

Despite their carnivorous diet, vulture bees produce honey through a process similar to nectar feeding bees. The bees gather meat particles and store them in their crop (honey stomach). Enzymes in the crop begin breaking down the meat proteins. The partially digested meat is regurgitated into honeycomb cells. Fanning wings create airflow to reduce moisture content. Microorganisms in the hive environment further break down the meat.

Alwy M. Jones

Contrary to expectations, vulture bee honey is described as clear and sweet, without any meat like qualities. This is due to the extensive breakdown of proteins during the production process.

Research by Jessica Maccaro et al. (2022) found that the gut microbiomes of vulture bees contain acid producing bacteria that likely play a role in breaking down carrion and producing palatable honey. The study, published in mBio, suggests that these bacteria may help neutralize toxins found in rotting meat.

Alwy M. Jones

The Massacre at Ayyadieh

In August 1191, during the Third Crusade, a shocking event occurred that would leave an indelible mark on the history of Christian-Muslim relations. King Richard I of England, known as Richard the Lionheart, ordered the massacre of approximately 2,700 Muslim prisoners at Ayyadieh, near Acre. This brutal act was ostensibly a response to the failure of Saladin, the Muslim leader, to meet ransom demands.

The Third Crusade (1189-1192) was launched in response to Saladin's capture of Jerusalem in 1187. Richard the Lionheart, along with other European monarchs, sought to reclaim the Holy Land for Christendom. The siege of Acre, a strategic port city, had been a prolonged affair, lasting from August 1189 to July 1191.

When Acre finally fell to the Crusaders on July 12th 1191, thousands of Muslim defenders were taken prisoner. Richard and Saladin entered into negotiations for their release, with Richard demanding a substantial ransom, the return of Christian prisoners, and the True Cross (a relic believed to be from Jesus' crucifixion).

As negotiations dragged on and deadlines passed without Saladin meeting the full terms, Richard grew impatient. On August 20th 1191, he ordered the execution of the Muslim prisoners. The massacre took place on a hill outside Acre, later named "Ayyadieh" or "Hill of Ayadiyya."

Contemporary accounts describe the scene as horrific, with Crusader knights and foot soldiers butchering the unarmed prisoners in full view of Saladin's army, which was camped nearby but unable to intervene.

Known for his military prowess, Richard's decision to execute the prisoners was likely a calculated move to demonstrate his ruthlessness and resolve. The Muslim leader was renowned for his chivalry and mercy. The massacre deeply affected him and influenced his subsequent treatment of Christian prisoners and civilians.

The massacre at Ayyadieh had significant repercussions; it set a precedent for increased brutality on both sides of the conflict. The massacre may have been intended to demoralize Saladin's forces, but it also hardened Muslim resistance. It severely damaged the possibility of negotiated settlements between Crusader and Muslim forces.

The massacre at Ayyadieh undermined any sense of shared chivalric code between the opposing forces. The event further entrenched religious hostilities, feeding into narratives of holy war on both sides. The massacre became a powerful symbol of Crusader cruelty in Muslim historiography, influencing perceptions for centuries to come. The event sparked discussions about the ethics of warfare and treatment of prisoners, themes that resonated throughout medieval literature and continue to be relevant today.

Alwy M. Jones

The Notorious Ruler of Wallachia

Vlad III, commonly known as Vlad the Impaler or Vlad Dracula, ruled Wallachia (part of present day Romania) from 1456 to 1462. His reign was marked by extreme cruelty, military prowess, and a fierce determination to protect his land from Ottoman expansion.

Born in 1431 in Sighişoara, Transylvania, Vlad was the second son of Vlad II Dracul, a member of the Order of the Dragon (Dracul). His early years were tumultuous, spent as a hostage of the Ottoman Empire alongside his younger brother, Radu. This experience likely shaped his future attitudes towards the Ottomans and his methods of rule.

Vlad ascended to the Wallachian throne in 1456, in a time of great political instability. His rule was characterized by; fierce opposition to Ottoman expansion, efforts to centralize power and reduce the influence of boyars (nobles), brutal punishment of criminals and enemies and military campaigns against Saxon merchants in Transylvania

Vlad earned his moniker "the Impaler" due to his preferred method of execution. Impalement was a gruesome process where victims were forced onto sharpened stakes and left to die slowly. This practice was used both as a method of punishment and as a psychological warfare tactic to terrify his enemies.

One of the most notorious events of Vlad's reign occurred in 1459 when a group of Ottoman envoys visited his court. According to historical accounts, these ambassadors refused to remove their turbans in Vlad's presence, citing religious custom. Vlad, perceiving this as a sign of disrespect, reportedly had their turbans nailed to their heads.

This incident is significant for several reasons; it demonstrates Vlad's ruthlessness and his willingness to flout diplomatic norms, showcases the cultural clash between Ottoman and European customs. The event served as a clear message to the Ottoman Empire about Vlad's stance towards their influence and it contributed significantly to Vlad's fearsome reputation both within Wallachia and beyond its borders.

Alwy M. Jones

Fowl Play

In an extraordinary turn of events that has left the local community both bewildered and fascinated, a court in Basel sentenced a chicken to death for the seemingly innocuous act of laying a brightly colored egg. The trial, which concluded yesterday, has drawn attention to the complex interplay between superstition, law, and justice in 15th century Europe.

The defendant, a common barnyard hen belonging to farmer Hans Mueller, stood accused of laying an egg of an unusually vivid hue. Witnesses described the egg as being a striking shade of red, a color associated with demonic influence in local folklore.

The trial, presided over by Magistrate Johann Schreiber, saw a parade of witnesses testifying to the unnatural color of the egg. Local priest Father Klaus Bauer provided expert testimony on the potential supernatural implications of such an occurrence.

Farmer Mueller, in a desperate attempt to save his hen, argued that the bird had simply eaten an unusual diet of berries, which might have affected the color of its eggs. However, his plea fell on deaf ears.

After deliberating for several hours, Magistrate Schreiber delivered the verdict; death by beheading. The sentence was to be carried out at dawn the following day in the town square.

The verdict sparked intense debate among the citizens of Basel. While some supported the court's decision, viewing it as necessary to ward off evil influences, others saw it as an overreaction fueled by superstition.

This case reflects the complex beliefs and fears prevalent in 15th century Europe. The period was marked by intense religious fervor, widespread superstition, and a deep-seated fear of supernatural influences. Animals were often viewed as potential vessels for demonic forces, leading to numerous trials of animals throughout Europe during this era.

Alwy M. Jones

The Spanish Inquisition

The Spanish Inquisition, established in 1478 and officially operating from 1481 to 1834, was a powerful institution created to maintain Catholic orthodoxy in the Spanish kingdoms.

The Spanish Inquisition was established by Catholic Monarchs Ferdinand II of Aragon and Isabella I of Castile, with the approval of Pope Sixtus IV. Its primary purpose was to ensure the orthodoxy of converts from Judaism and Islam, known as conversos and moriscos, respectively. The Inquisition was also tasked with rooting out heresy and maintaining the supremacy of the Catholic faith in Spain.

Key features of the Spanish Inquisition included; centralized authority under the Spanish monarchy, unlike earlier medieval inquisitions, jurisdiction over all Spanish territories, including colonies and power to investigate, try, and punish individuals suspected of heresy.

The Inquisition primarily focused on; Jews who had converted to Christianity but were suspected of secretly practicing Judaism, Muslims who had converted to Christianity but were suspected of maintaining Islamic practices, Protestants and other Christian sects deemed heretical and individuals accused of blasphemy, witchcraft, or moral crimes.

The Inquisition employed various methods to identify and prosecute suspected heretics; encouragement of people to report suspected heretics, questioning of suspects and witnesses, torture used to extract confessions, though its use was regulated and public ritual of sentencing and punishment, including executions.

Alwy M. Jones

Marsilio Ficino and the Historical Practice of Hematophagy

The consumption of human blood as a form of medicine, while shocking to modern sensibilities, was not uncommon in certain periods of history.

Marsilio Ficino, a prominent Neoplatonist philosopher and physician, wrote extensively on the subject of prolonging life and maintaining youth. In his work "De Vita Libri Tres" (Three Books on Life), published in 1489, Ficino suggested that the consumption of young blood could have rejuvenating effects on the elderly. He wrote:

"Why shouldn't our old people, namely those who have no [other] recourse, likewise suck the blood of a youth? A youth who is willing, healthy, happy, and temperate, whose blood is of the best but perhaps too abundant. They will suck like leeches, an ounce or two from a scarcely opened vein of the left arm; then they will immediately drink it while it is still warm."

This recommendation was based on the belief that blood from young, healthy individuals contained vital spirits that could be transferred to the elderly, reinvigorating their bodies and minds.

To understand Ficino's recommendation, it's crucial to consider the prevailing medical theories of his time. Renaissance medicine was still heavily influenced by the Galenic tradition and the theory of the four humors: blood, phlegm, yellow bile, and black bile.

Blood was considered the most important humor, associated with warmth, moisture, and vitality.

The concept of "vital spirits" was central to this understanding of physiology. These spirits were thought to be produced in the heart and carried throughout the body by the blood. As people aged, it was believed that their vital spirits diminished, leading to physical and mental decline. The consumption of young blood was seen as a way to replenish these vital spirits directly.

The idea of consuming blood for medicinal purposes was not unique to Ficino or the Renaissance. Various cultures throughout history have practiced forms of hematophagy for perceived health benefits. Ancient Romans drank the blood of gladiators to cure epilepsy. In medieval Europe, blood was sometimes used as a treatment for leprosy.

Alwy M. Jones

A Royal Agony

Gout, a form of inflammatory arthritis caused by excess uric acid in the blood, has plagued humanity for millennia. The Tudor era (1485-1603) in England was no exception, with its fair share of gout ridden monarchs and nobles. However, the treatments employed during this period differed greatly from our modern understanding of medicine, offering a fascinating glimpse into the beliefs and practices of the time.

Tudor medicine was heavily influenced by the ancient Greek theory of humors. This theory posited that the human body was composed of four fluids; blood, yellow bile, black bile, and phlegm, and good health depended on their balance. Gout, according to this view, arose from an excess of black bile, causing a buildup of toxins that manifested as painful inflammation in the joints, particularly the big toe.

Faced with such discomfort, Tudor sufferers sought a variety of remedies, some more bizarre than others. One such treatment involved boiling a red-haired dog in oil, worms, and pig marrow. The rationale behind this gruesome concoction likely stemmed from the "doctrine of signatures," a belief that the physical characteristics of a plant or animal held clues to its medicinal properties. The fiery red hair of the dog was perhaps seen as a way to counteract the perceived "coldness" of black bile.

Herbs played a significant role in Tudor medicine, and gout was no exception. Colchicum autumnale, the source of the modern gout medication colchicine, was known even then and used to reduce inflammation. Other herbs, like meadowsweet and nettle, were believed to have diuretic properties, aiming to flush out excess uric acid. Bloodletting, a common practice for various ailments, was also employed for gout, with the belief that removing some blood would help restore the balance of humors.

The effectiveness of these treatments was, at best, questionable. Boiling a dog in oil would have offered little to no medical benefit, and the potential for infection from such practices was high. Bloodletting could weaken patients and further complicate their health. The "doctrine of signatures" often led to bizarre and ineffective concoctions, highlighting the limitations of medical knowledge at the time.

The Reign of "Bloody Mary"

Mary I, daughter of Henry VIII and Catherine of Aragon, ascended to the English throne in 1553, becoming the first undisputed Queen regnant of England. Her five year reign was marked by attempts to reverse the English Reformation and restore Roman Catholicism as the state religion, earning her the posthumous nickname "Bloody Mary" due to her persecution of Protestants.

Mary's accession followed a brief struggle with supporters of Lady Jane Grey, who had been named heir by Mary's half-brother, Edward VI. Upon securing the throne, Mary immediately set about reversing the Protestant reforms implemented during Edward's reign.

Mary's religious policy included; repealing anti-Catholic legislation passed under Henry VIII and Edward VI, restoring the heresy laws, reuniting the Church of England with Rome and reintroducing Catholic practices and doctrines.

Mary's most controversial actions were the executions of Protestant dissenters, known as the Marian Persecutions. Over the course of her reign, more than 280 religious dissenters were burned at the stake, including prominent Protestant leaders such as Thomas Cranmer, Hugh Latimer, and Nicholas Ridley.

While the number of executions under Mary was not unprecedented for the time (her father, Henry VIII, had executed significantly more people), the public nature of the burnings and the religious motivation behind them left a lasting impact on English public opinion.

Mary's actions must be understood within the context of 16th century Europe, where religious uniformity was seen as essential for political stability. Many European rulers of the time, both Catholic and Protestant, persecuted religious dissenters. Marriage to Philip II of Spain in 1554, which was unpopular among the English people. Loss of Calais, England's last continental possession, to France in 1558. Economic difficulties, including inflation and poor harvests.

Alwy M. Jones

The St. Bartholomew's Day Massacre

On August 24th 1572, France witnessed one of the most brutal episodes in its history; the St. Bartholomew's Day massacre. This event, which saw the mass killing of Huguenots (French Protestants) in Paris and throughout France, marked a pivotal moment in the French Wars of Religion and had far reaching consequences for European politics and religion.

The massacre occurred against the backdrop of the French Wars of Religion (1562-1598), a series of conflicts between Catholics and Protestants in France. The country was deeply divided along religious lines, with the Catholic majority led by the powerful Guise family, while the Protestant minority, known as Huguenots, was led by the Bourbon family.

The growing Protestant movement was seen as a threat to Catholic dominance. The weakening of the Valois monarchy led to increased competition among noble factions. The marriage of Margaret of Valois to Henry of Navarre; this union between a Catholic princess and a Protestant leader was intended to ease tensions but instead heightened suspicions.

The violence began in Paris on the night of August 23rd -24th 1572, coinciding with the feast of St. Bartholomew. The initial target was Admiral Gaspard de Coligny, a prominent Huguenot leader, who had been wounded in an assassination attempt days earlier. The killing quickly spread to other Huguenot leaders and then to the general Protestant population.

Admiral Coligny was murdered in his bed. The Paris mob, incited by Catholic leaders, began indiscriminately killing Protestants. The violence spread to other French cities over the following weeks. Estimates of the death toll vary widely, with some contemporary sources claiming up to 70,000 deaths. Modern historians generally estimate the number to be between 5,000 and 30,000.

Alwy M. Jones

The Golden Tutor of Mughal Princes

In the vibrant tapestry of Mughal India, few figures stand out as prominently as Abu'l-Fazl ibn Mubarak, the renowned Persian poet, historian, and tutor to Emperor Akbar's sons. For 15 years, from approximately 1575 to 1590, Abu'l-Fazl held the esteemed position of personal instructor to the imperial princes, shaping the minds of future rulers and leaving an indelible mark on Mughal history.

Abu'l-Fazl was entrusted with the education of Akbar's three sons:

1. Prince Salim (later Emperor Jahangir)

2. Prince Murad

3. Prince Daniyal

Each prince brought unique challenges and opportunities to the role of tutor, requiring Abu'l-Fazl to tailor his approach to their individual temperaments and abilities.

Perhaps the most intriguing aspect of Abu'l-Fazl's tenure was his unprecedented compensation arrangement. Each year, he received a payment in gold equal to the combined weight of his three royal students.

The arrangement potentially incentivized Abu'l-Fazl to ensure the princes' physical health and growth, as their increasing weight directly correlated with his income.

The sheer extravagance of the payment underscored the immense value Akbar placed on his sons' education and on Abu'l-Fazl's services. This generous compensation provided Abu'l-Fazl with significant wealth, allowing him to focus entirely on his scholarly and tutoring duties.

The Mughal court was known for its lavish patronage of arts and sciences. Abu'l-Fazl's compensation exemplified this tradition, elevating the status of education to that of other highly prized courtly arts. The arrangement reflected Akbar's deep appreciation for knowledge and his commitment to providing the best possible education for his heirs. Akbar's reign was marked by efforts to promote talent regardless of background. Abu'l-Fazl, rising to such a prestigious position based on his intellectual abilities, embodied this meritocratic ideal.

Alwy M. Jones

The Sawney Bean Clan

The tale of Sawney Bean and his cannibalistic family is one of the most gruesome and controversial stories in Scottish folklore. Allegedly taking place during the reign of King James VI of Scotland (later James I of England) in the late 16th century, this macabre account has captivated and horrified audiences for centuries. While the historical accuracy of the story is debated, its impact on Scottish culture and folklore is undeniable.

Scotland in the late 16th century was a country marked by political instability, religious conflict, and economic hardship. The Scottish Reformation had recently taken place, and tensions between Catholics and Protestants were high. Rural areas were often lawless, with bandits and outlaws taking advantage of the lack of centralized authority. It was in this tumultuous environment that the story of Sawney Bean and his clan is said to have unfolded. According to the legend, Alexander "Sawney" Bean was born in East Lothian, near Edinburgh. Rejecting his father's honest trade as a ditch digger and hedge trimmer, Sawney left home with a woman who would become his wife and partner in crime. The couple settled in a remote coastal cave in Bennane Head, Ayrshire, which would become their base of operations for the next 25 years.

Over time, Sawney and his wife had eight sons, six daughters, and through incest, 32 grandchildren. This inbred clan, cut off from society, turned to robbery and murder to sustain themselves.

The Bean clan's modus operandi was to ambush travelers on nearby roads, usually at night. Their victims were dragged back to the cave, where they were murdered, dismembered, and cannibalized. Parts of the bodies were pickled for later consumption, while any remaining evidence was disposed of in the sea. According to the legend, the clan was responsible for the disappearance of over 1,000 people over their quarter century reign of terror. The sheer number of missing persons caused panic in the surrounding communities, with locals afraid to travel, especially after dark.

According to the legend, the Bean clan's downfall came when they attacked a couple returning from a local fair. The man, a skilled fighter, managed to fend off the attackers long enough for a large group of fair-goers to come to their aid. This incident finally brought the clan's activities to light.

King James VI allegedly led a manhunt of 400 men and bloodhounds to track down the Beans. The search party eventually discovered the clan's cave, filled with human remains and stolen goods. The entire Bean family was captured and taken to Edinburgh for execution without trial.

> The men of the clan were allegedly dismembered and left to bleed to death, mirroring their treatment of victims. The women and children were said to have been burned alive.

Alwy M. Jones

Archbishop James Ussher's Monumental Calculation

In 1654, Irish Archbishop James Ussher made a bold proclamation that would echo through centuries of theological, scientific, and historical discourse. According to Ussher's meticulous calculations, the universe was created on Sunday, October 21st 4004 BC, at precisely 9:00 in the morning. This audacious claim, born from a blend of biblical scholarship and historical research, would have far-reaching implications for how people understood the age of the Earth and the timeline of human existence.

The Church still held significant sway over intellectual pursuits, with the Bible considered the ultimate authority on history and natural phenomena. The 17th century saw the birth of modern scientific methods, with figures like Galileo and Newton challenging traditional views. Scholars were increasingly interested in establishing precise historical timelines, often blending biblical and secular sources. As a Protestant archbishop, Ussher was part of a movement that emphasized direct interpretation of scripture.

Archbishop Ussher's calculation was not a mere guess but the result of years of painstaking research and analysis. Ussher meticulously traced the genealogies presented in the Old Testament, calculating the years between generations. He correlated biblical events with known historical occurrences from other ancient civilizations.

Ussher used knowledge of ancient and medieval calendars to align biblical chronology with astronomical events, he took the Bible's seven days of creation literally, assuming no gaps or metaphorical time periods. Ussher believed that God would have created the world on a Sunday, the first day of the week, and at the autumnal equinox.

Alwy M. Jones

The Great Bullion Transfer

Between 1500 and 1650, Spanish conquistadors orchestrated one of the most significant transfers of wealth in human history. An estimated 180 tonnes (400,000 pounds) of gold and 16,000 tonnes (3.5 million pounds) of silver were shipped from the Americas to Europe. This massive influx of precious metals had far reaching consequences, reshaping the economic, social, and political landscapes of both the Old and New Worlds.

The sudden increase in gold and silver supply led to significant inflation across Europe, known as the "Price Revolution." Prices rose by 200 - 400% over the 150 year period. The abundance of precious metals stimulated international trade, particularly with Asia, as Europeans now had more purchasing power for exotic goods. The influx of bullion contributed to the growth of banking systems and new financial instruments to manage the increased wealth. Spain briefly became the wealthiest nation in Europe, although much of the wealth quickly dispersed to other countries due to Spain's reliance on imports. The inflation weakened the economic basis of feudalism, as fixed rents became less valuable over time.

In Europe, the inflation led to a decline in the relative wealth of the landed aristocracy and a rise of the merchant class. The economic boom led to increased urbanization in Europe as people moved to cities for new economic opportunities. In the Americas, the demand for labor in mines led to the exploitation and decimation of indigenous populations. The need for labor in American mines and plantations fueled the transatlantic slave trade, with profound and lasting social impacts.

The wealth from the Americas helped finance the rise of centralized nation states in Europe, particularly Spain. The success of Spanish colonization spurred other European powers to seek their own colonies, leading to global imperial competition. The increased wealth allowed European monarchs to finance larger armies and more prolonged conflicts. The transfer of wealth contributed to the shift of global economic and political power from Asia to Europe.

The combination of disease, warfare, and harsh labor conditions led to a catastrophic decline in indigenous populations. Many indigenous cultures and knowledge systems were destroyed or suppressed by the conquistadors. The Americas were integrated into a global economic system as producers of raw materials and precious metals.

Alwy M. Jones

The Heart of the Sun King

The story of Louis XIV's heart is a fascinating journey through French history, touching on royal tradition, revolutionary fervor, and Victorian eccentricity.

Louis XIV, known as the Sun King, ruled France from 1643 to 1715. Upon his death, his body was subject to the traditional embalming practices reserved for French monarchs.

The body was divided, with the heart and entrails removed for separate preservation. The heart was treated with spirits of wine, spices, and preservative compounds. Placement in a heart shaped lead casket, this was then encased in a silver gilt container.

The preservation of royal hearts was a long standing tradition in France, symbolizing the monarch's eternal love for their subjects and ensuring their spiritual presence even after death.

The heart of Louis XIV held immense cultural and political significance; it represented the doctrine that monarchs were God's representatives on Earth. The heart served as a rallying point for royalist sentiment. It was a tangible link to one of the most influential periods in French history.

The heart was initially kept at the Church of the Jesuits (now Saint Paul Saint Louis) in Paris, where it was an object of veneration and historical interest.

The French Revolution, beginning in 1789, saw a dramatic shift in attitudes towards the monarchy. In 1793, during the height of revolutionary fervor; revolutionaries targeted symbols of royal power, including Louis XIV's heart. The lead casket containing the heart was stolen from the church. The exact circumstances of the theft remain unclear, but it was likely part of a wider campaign to eradicate royalist symbols. The theft of the heart was both a practical act of revolutionary zeal and a symbolic rejection of monarchical authority.

After its theft, the heart of Louis XIV disappeared from historical record for several decades. Its fate remained a mystery, fueling speculation and legend.

In the 19th century, a peculiar rumor emerged concerning the fate of Louis XIV's heart. This rumor centered around William Buckland, an English geologist and paleontologist known for his eccentricities. Buckland was said to have a penchant for zoophagy (eating unusual animals). According to the story, Buckland attended a dinner party where a small, mummified heart was presented. The heart was purported to be that of Louis XIV. Buckland, true to his reputation, allegedly ate the heart.

Alwy M. Jones

Biological Warfare in Colonial America

The use of disease as a weapon of war is a dark chapter in human history, and one of the earliest documented attempts in North America occurred in 1758 during the French and Indian War.

The incident took place during the French and Indian War (1754-1763), part of the larger Seven Years' War. Britain and France were competing for control of North America. Many Native American tribes allied with the French against the British. The event occurred during Pontiac's War, a Native American uprising against British colonial expansion.

In June 1763, during the siege of Fort Pitt (modern day Pittsburgh, Pennsylvania), British forces led by General Jeffrey Amherst and Colonel Henry Bouquet discussed using smallpox as a weapon against the Native Americans. The key events were:

Amherst wrote to Bouquet, suggesting the use of smallpox against the Native Americans. Two blankets and a handkerchief from the fort's smallpox hospital were given to Native American delegates during negotiations. The transfer of these items was recorded in the fort's logbook by William Trent, a local trader.

The British forces had several motivations for considering this tactic; weakening the Native American forces besieging Fort Pitt, removing Native American resistance to British colonial expansion, prevailing racist views that dehumanized Native

Americans and the siege had put the British forces in a precarious position.

A smallpox epidemic did occur among the Ohio Valley tribes shortly after the incident. Thousands of Native Americans died in the subsequent outbreak, though it's unclear how many cases were directly related to the Fort Pitt incident. The epidemic contributed to the disruption of Native American societies and their ability to resist colonial expansion.

A Pivotal Moment in American Expansion

The Louisiana Purchase of 1803 stands as one of the most significant land acquisitions in United States history. This monumental deal between the United States and France not only doubled the size of the young nation but also set the stage for westward expansion and the fulfillment of the concept of Manifest Destiny.

At the turn of the 19th century, the United States was a fledgling nation confined to the eastern seaboard. The vast territory of Louisiana, stretching from the Mississippi River to the Rocky Mountains, was under French control. However, France, under Napoleon Bonaparte, faced challenges in Europe and saw the American continent as a secondary priority.

Key players:

- Thomas Jefferson: President of the United States

- James Monroe and Robert Livingston: U.S. negotiators

- Napoleon Bonaparte: First Consul of France

Initially, Jefferson sought only to purchase New Orleans and parts of the Florida territory to secure American access to the Mississippi River. However, Napoleon, needing funds for his European campaigns, offered the entire Louisiana territory.

Key details of the purchase:

- Date: April 30, 1803

- Total cost: $15 million (approximately $340 million in 2021 dollars)

- Price per acre: Roughly 4 cents

- Size of territory: Approximately 828,000 square miles (2.14 million square kilometers)

The negotiation process was remarkably swift, with the entire deal concluded in a matter of weeks. This speed was due in part to Napoleon's urgency to sell and the American negotiators' recognition of the extraordinary opportunity.

Jefferson saw the purchase as a way to secure America's western frontier and promote agrarian democracy. Many Americans viewed it as a step towards fulfilling the nation's destiny to span the continent.

Napoleon saw the sale as a way to finance his European military campaigns. He also hoped to check British power by strengthening the United States.

Manifest Destiny fueled the ideology of American expansion across the continent. The purchase led to increased pressure on Native American lands and cultures. The new territories became a focal point in debates over the expansion of slavery. Access to new resources and trade routes spurred American economic development.

Alwy M. Jones

A Legacy of Inhumanity and Controversy

Andrew Jackson, the seventh President of the United States (1829-1837), is a complex and controversial figure in American history. Known for his military prowess and populist policies, Jackson's presidency marked a significant shift in American politics. However, his legacy is deeply tarnished by his inhumane treatment of enslaved people and Native Americans, actions that continue to spark debate and criticism to this day.

Jackson was a lifelong slave owner, possessing over 150 enslaved individuals at the time of his death. His plantation, The Hermitage, was built and maintained through slave labor. Jackson's views on slavery were typical of many Southern plantation owners of his time, he saw it as an economic necessity and a natural part of the social order. He frequently placed ads for runaway slaves, offering rewards for their capture and return. There are accounts of harsh punishments, including whipping, for slaves who attempted to escape. In 1804, Jackson bought an enslaved woman named Hannah and her child. The advertisement described her as "breeding" stock, highlighting the dehumanizing nature of the slave trade.

During his presidency, Jackson's policies generally favored the continuation and expansion of slavery. He opposed abolitionist movements and supported the gag rule that tabled anti-slavery petitions in Congress without discussion.

Jackson's policies towards Native Americans were arguably his most egregious acts of inhumanity. The Indian Removal Act of 1830, which he championed and signed into law, authorized the president to negotiate treaties to buy tribal lands in the east in exchange for lands further west. This act led to the forced relocation of tens of thousands of Native Americans.

The most infamous consequence of this policy was the Trail of Tears, the forced relocation of Cherokee, Muscogee, Seminole, Chickasaw, and Choctaw nations from their ancestral homelands in the Southeastern United States to areas west of the Mississippi River. This journey resulted in the deaths of thousands due to exposure, disease, and starvation.

Jackson personally negotiated several treaties that dispossessed Native American tribes of their lands. He ignored a Supreme Court ruling (Worcester v. Georgia, 1832) that affirmed Cherokee sovereignty, famously saying, "John Marshall has made his decision; now let him enforce it!" He used military force to remove tribes that resisted relocation, leading to conflicts such as the Second Seminole War.

Jackson's legacy has become increasingly contentious in recent years. While he was long celebrated as a war hero and champion of the common man, modern historians and the public have become more critical of his actions, particularly regarding slavery and Native American removal.

Alwy M. Jones

America's Dark Legacy

Inhumanity, defined as extreme cruelty and a lack of compassion for fellow human beings, finds one of its most egregious expressions in the institution of slavery. In the United States, slavery and its aftermath, including the Jim Crow era, represent a long and painful chapter of history characterized by systemic oppression and racial discrimination.

Slavery in America began in the early 17th century with the arrival of the first enslaved Africans in the Virginia colony in 1619. The transatlantic slave trade, which forcibly transported millions of Africans to the Americas, was driven by economic motivations, particularly the labor intensive cultivation of crops like tobacco, cotton, and sugar. By 1790, the first U.S. Census recorded nearly 700,000 enslaved individuals, representing about 18% of the total population. This number grew to nearly 4 million by 1860, on the eve of the Civil War. The social implications of enslaving African people were profound. It led to the development of racist ideologies to justify the practice, creating a hierarchical society based on race that would persist long after slavery's abolition.

Enslaved people were often housed in overcrowded, unsanitary quarters with inadequate food and clothing. Families were routinely torn apart through sales, with an estimated 1 in 3 enslaved individuals in the Upper South sold away from their families. Whippings, brandings, and other forms of corporal punishment were common. Enslaved women were frequently subjected to rape and sexual abuse by slave owners. Many states passed laws prohibiting the education of enslaved individuals, fearing literacy would lead to rebellion.

Despite these conditions, enslaved individuals resisted in various ways, from small acts of defiance to organized rebellions like Nat Turner's in 1831.

Following the Civil War and the abolition of slavery, the brief period of Reconstruction (1865-1877) saw significant gains in civil rights for African Americans. However, these advances were short lived. As Reconstruction ended, Southern states began enacting laws to reassert white supremacy and disenfranchise African Americans. These Jim Crow laws, named after a racist caricature, were a system of state and local statutes that enforced racial segregation and codified black Americans as second class citizens. The 1896 Supreme Court decision in Plessy v. Ferguson, which upheld the constitutionality of racial segregation under the "separate but equal" doctrine, gave legal sanction to Jim Crow. Public spaces, including schools, transportation, and businesses, were strictly segregated. Voting restrictions, including literacy tests and poll taxes, effectively denied African Americans the right to vote. Job discrimination and limited educational opportunities perpetuated cycles of poverty. Lynching and other forms of racial terror were used to enforce the Jim Crow system. Between 1882 and 1968, an estimated 4,743 lynching occurred in the United States, with the majority of victims being African American.

William Henry Harrison

William Henry Harrison's presidency, though incredibly brief, was a significant moment in American history that highlighted the fragility of leadership succession and had lasting impacts on the political landscape of the 19th century. Harrison, born in 1773, was a military hero known for his victory at the Battle of Tippecanoe in 1811. He leveraged this fame in his successful 1840 presidential campaign, running as the Whig Party candidate with John Tyler as his vice president. The campaign, famously dubbed the "Log Cabin and Hard Cider" campaign, portrayed Harrison as a man of the people, contrasting him with the incumbent Democrat Martin Van Buren.

Harrison's inauguration on March 4th 1841, was notable for two reasons. First, at 68, he was the oldest president elected to that point. Second, he delivered the longest inaugural address in history, speaking for nearly two hours in cold, wet weather without a coat or hat. This decision would prove fateful.

Shortly after his inauguration, Harrison fell ill with what was likely pneumonia. Despite efforts to treat him, he died on April 4th 1841, just 31 days into his term. He became the first U.S. president to die in office.

Alwy M. Jones

The 'Dirtiest Man in England' and a Victorian Spectacle

In the annals of Victorian England, few figures captured the public imagination quite like James Lucas, infamously known as the 'dirtiest man in England'. His extreme aversion to cleanliness and the resulting spectacle of his appearance made him a subject of both fascination and revulsion, drawing curious onlookers from far and wide. James Lucas, born in the early 19th century, lived in Broadward Hall, Shropshire. Following a family dispute in his youth, Lucas withdrew from society and developed an intense aversion to personal hygiene. Over decades, his body underwent a startling transformation due to his refusal to wash. Lucas's appearance was nothing short of terrifying to Victorian sensibilities. His skin was said to be encrusted with a thick layer of grime, his hair and beard matted into a solid mass. His nails grew long and twisted, and his clothes, never changed, rotted on his body. The accumulation of dirt and debris gave him an almost inhuman appearance, more akin to a creature of folklore than a man.

The Victorian era was marked by a fascination with the unusual and the grotesque, and James Lucas became a prime example of this cultural phenomenon. People would travel great distances to catch a glimpse of the 'dirtiest man in England'. Some accounts suggest that visitors would leave gifts of food and alcohol for Lucas, perhaps in exchange for the chance to see him.

Alwy M. Jones

The Unsung Heroes of Hygiene

The narrative of hygiene often centers on European advancements, overlooking the significant contributions of African cultures. Centuries before the European Renaissance, African societies had developed sophisticated practices for maintaining health and preventing diseases. Many African cultures placed a strong emphasis on cleanliness and personal hygiene. Regular bathing and washing were common practices, often incorporated into daily routines and religious rituals. For instance, the ancient Egyptians were meticulous about personal hygiene, using water, oils, and perfumes for bathing and grooming. They also developed intricate systems for water purification and sanitation, including advanced sewage systems. Beyond personal cleanliness, African societies demonstrated an understanding of environmental hygiene. Proper waste disposal, the construction of latrines, and the management of water sources were integral parts of community life. These practices significantly reduced the risk of waterborne diseases.

The interactions between Africa and Europe during the medieval and early modern periods facilitated the transfer of knowledge, including hygiene practices. The Moorish occupation of the Iberian Peninsula introduced Europeans to advanced techniques in sanitation, personal hygiene, and healthcare. Arab scholars, drawing on African and Middle Eastern knowledge, translated and disseminated works on medicine and hygiene.

Moreover, the transatlantic slave trade, while a horrific chapter in history, inadvertently contributed to the spread of hygiene practices. Enslaved Africans brought their knowledge of sanitation, herbal remedies, and disease prevention to the Americas and Europe. For example, the cultivation of cotton, a staple crop in Africa, introduced Europeans to new fiber-based hygiene products. The influx of African hygiene practices coincided with a period of significant change in Europe. The Black Death, a devastating pandemic, highlighted the urgent need for improved sanitation and personal hygiene. The adoption of African inspired practices, such as regular bathing and washing, contributed to a gradual decline in disease prevalence.

Furthermore, the introduction of African medicinal plants and herbal remedies enriched European pharmacopoeia. Many of these plants, such as aloe vera and baobab, are now widely used in modern medicine. The exchange of knowledge also stimulated advancements in European medical science, leading to the development of new treatments and preventive measures. The adoption of African hygiene practices contributed to a shift in European societal norms, emphasizing cleanliness and personal care. These changes laid the foundation for modern public health systems and influenced the development of healthcare infrastructure. Moreover, the recognition of Africa's contributions to global health has fostered a renewed interest in traditional African medicine and its potential to address contemporary health challenges.

Alwy M. Jones

A Historical Lens on Hygiene and Public Health

Typhus, a group of infectious diseases caused by Rickettsia bacteria, has played a significant role in shaping public health history. Typhus, also known as "jail fever" or "war fever," which has been responsible for millions of deaths throughout history. Typhus is primarily spread by body lice and thrives in conditions of poor hygiene and overcrowding, making it a potent threat during times of social upheaval and conflict.

Typhus has been a scourge of humanity for centuries, with major outbreaks occurring during:

- The Napoleonic Wars (1803-1815): Typhus decimated Napoleon's army during the retreat from Moscow in 1812.

- The Irish Potato Famine (1845-1849): Over 100,000 people died from typhus during this period.

- World War I (1914-1918): Millions were affected, particularly on the Eastern Front.

- World War II (1939-1945): Outbreaks were common in concentration camps and ghettos.

These outbreaks were exacerbated by socio-economic conditions such as poverty, displacement, and war, which led to overcrowding and deteriorating sanitary conditions.

Poor hygiene practices were prevalent during typhus outbreaks, contributing significantly to the spread of the disease. Lack of access to clean water made regular washing difficult or impossible. Human and animal waste often accumulated in living areas. Close quarters in tenements, prisons, and refugee camps facilitated lice transmission.

The connection between sanitation and typhus became increasingly clear in the 19th century. In 1847, William Budd demonstrated the link between body lice and typhus transmission, highlighting the importance of personal cleanliness in disease prevention.

In many parts of Europe, frequent bathing was not common practice until the late 19th century. Some religious groups viewed excessive bathing as a form of vanity or moral laxity. Many urban dwellers lacked access to private bathing facilities.

For example, in Victorian England, the working class often bathed only once a week, if at all. This infrequency allowed body lice to thrive, increasing the risk of typhus transmission.

Alwy M. Jones

A Taste of Natural History

In the annals of 19th century natural history, few figures stand out quite like William Buckland and his son Frank. While their contributions to paleontology and zoology are well documented, it's their unconventional dietary habits that truly capture the imagination. From stewed flies to mice on toast, the Bucklands' culinary explorations pushed the boundaries of both science and gastronomy.

William Buckland (1784-1856) was a prominent English geologist and paleontologist, best known for his work on fossil remains and his role in developing the field of geology. His son, Frank Buckland (1826-1880), followed in his father's footsteps, becoming a noted surgeon, zoologist, and natural historian.

Both men were driven by an insatiable curiosity about the natural world, which extended to a desire to understand the edibility and nutritional value of various animals, including those not typically considered food in Western culture.

The Bucklands' dietary experiments were extensive and often bizarre by contemporary standards. William Buckland reportedly consumed flies stewed in butter, claiming they tasted similar to partridge. Frank Buckland experimented with various preparations of mice, including serving them on toast. The Bucklands sampled mole, finding it had an earthy flavor but was generally unpalatable due to its strong scent glands.

Frank once dined on panther meat, describing it as tough but flavorful. Both Bucklands sampled crocodile meat, with Frank noting its similarity to veal. During his time at Oxford, William reportedly served elephant trunk soup to his students.

Alwy M. Jones

The British Response to the Indian Mutiny of 1857

The Indian Mutiny of 1857, also known as the Sepoy Rebellion or the First War of Indian Independence, marked a watershed moment in the history of British colonial rule in India. The British response to this uprising was characterized by extreme brutality, with one of the most infamous punishments being the use of cannon firing to execute rebellious Indian soldiers.

The mutiny began in May 1857 when Indian soldiers (sepoys) in the British East India Company's army rebelled against their British officers. The immediate trigger was the rumored use of animal fat in the grease for new rifle cartridges, which offended both Hindu and Muslim sepoys. However, the underlying causes were much deeper, including resentment against British cultural and religious impositions, land annexations, and general discontent with colonial rule.

As the rebellion spread across northern and central India, the British response was swift and severe. Determined to crush the uprising and reassert their authority, British forces employed a range of punitive measures.

Cannon firing executions; known as "blowing from guns," involved tying condemned rebels to the mouths of cannons and firing them, resulting in a gruesome and public death. Mass hangings and firing squads; large numbers of suspected rebels were executed through more conventional means. Entire villages suspected of harboring rebels were burned to the ground. Communities were held responsible for individual acts of rebellion, leading to widespread reprisals.

Cannon-firing as Punishment method of execution was deeply offensive to both Hindu and Muslim beliefs about the treatment of the dead, adding religious insult to physical injury.

Alwy M. Jones

The Siege of Paris

The Siege of Paris, lasting from September 19th 1870, to January 28th 1871, during the Franco Prussian War, was a period of extreme hardship for the city's residents. As Prussian forces surrounded the French capital, cutting off supply lines, Parisians faced an unprecedented food shortage that would test their resilience and challenge societal norms.

As the siege began, Paris had approximately two million inhabitants, including refugees from surrounding areas. Initially, the city had food stocks for about two months, but as the siege dragged on, these supplies quickly dwindled. The government rationed bread, meat, and fuel, but these measures proved insufficient as winter approached.

As traditional food sources became scarce, Parisians turned to unconventional alternatives. The animals in the Jardin des Plantes zoo, including two elephants named Castor and Pollux, were slaughtered for meat. Pets; dogs, cats, and even pet birds became a source of protein. Contemporary accounts suggest that cat meat sold for 6 francs per kilo, while dog meat fetched 2 francs. Rats, abundant in the sewers of Paris, became a prized commodity. Restaurants even featured "rat pate" on their menus. An estimated 65,000 horses were consumed during the siege, starting with workhorses and eventually including prized racehorses.

The consumption of these unconventional food sources had profound social and cultural impacts. While the poor resorted to eating rats and stray animals, the wealthy could still afford luxury items at exorbitant prices. This disparity heightened existing class tensions. Chefs in Paris developed new recipes to make unpalatable meats more appealing. The siege gave birth to dishes like "rat a la Robert" and "cat en civet." The necessity of eating pets and vermin challenged long held cultural taboos about what constituted acceptable food. The stress of food scarcity and the consumption of pets took a significant psychological toll on the population.

Primary sources provide vivid descriptions of life during the siege. In his diary, Edmond de Goncourt wrote on Christmas Day, 1870; "People are beginning to eat dogs, cats, and rats. At the butcher Debacq's in the Rue de Seine, they are selling horse meat, donkey, mule, cat, and dog."

Victor Hugo, in a letter dated December 12th 1870, noted;

"We are eating the unknown... I am determined to try rat. The people are eating horse. I am eating horse. I will eat rat."

Alwy M. Jones

Public Beheadings on Amak and Moen

In the 19th century, the Danish islands of Amak (Amager) and Moen were the sites of public beheadings that drew large crowds, not only for the macabre spectacle but also for a peculiar medicinal purpose. These events provide a window into the complex interplay of justice, entertainment, and folk medicine in Danish society of the time.

Public executions were common throughout Europe in the 19th century, and Denmark was no exception. On Amak and Moen, beheadings were carried out in open spaces, often on hills or in town squares, to accommodate the substantial crowds that would gather. These events were seen as both a deterrent to crime and a form of public entertainment.

The executions were typically scheduled well in advance, allowing news to spread and attracting spectators from surrounding areas. Contemporary accounts describe a carnival like atmosphere, with vendors selling food and drink, and people of all social classes in attendance.

Perhaps the most striking aspect of these public beheadings was the presence of individuals suffering from epilepsy. A widespread folk belief of the time held that the blood of an executed criminal possessed powerful medicinal properties, particularly for treating epilepsy.

As a result, people with epilepsy, often accompanied by family members, would gather around the scaffold with cups or vials. Their goal was to collect the blood of the condemned as it flowed from the severed neck, believing that drinking this blood would cure their condition.

Understanding of epilepsy was rudimentary, and effective treatments were scarce. This vacuum was often filled by folk remedies and superstitions. The lack of effective medical treatments meant that people were willing to try extreme measures, even those that might seem gruesome by modern standards. The idea that criminal blood held curative powers may have been linked to religious concepts of sacrifice and redemption. The willingness of authorities to allow this practice suggests a degree of acceptance or at least tolerance for folk medicine alongside more official treatments.

The belief in the curative power of executed criminals' blood was not unique to Denmark. Similar practices were recorded in other parts of Europe, including Germany and England. The specific reasoning behind this belief varied. Blood was seen as the essence of life, and criminal blood was thought to possess a potent life force. Some believed that the strength and vitality of the criminal could be transferred to the epileptic through the blood. There was a notion that the shock of consuming such a powerful substance could "reset" the nervous system and cure epilepsy.

Alwy M. Jones

The Great Cat Mummy Mystery

In 1888, an Egyptian farmer's shovel struck something unusual in the sun baked earth near the village of Beni Hassan. Little did he know that his discovery would unearth one of the most fascinating and controversial chapters in the history of Egyptology; the great cat cemetery of Bubastis.

As the farmer's shovel broke through the ground, he revealed a vast underground chamber filled with countless mummified cats. The sight must have been both awe, inspiring and eerie; thousands of feline shapes, carefully wrapped and preserved, their silent forms a testament to the ancient Egyptians' reverence for these enigmatic creatures.

Experts estimate that the cemetery contained between 80,000 to 300,000 cat mummies. This staggering number highlights the immense scale of cat worship in ancient Egypt and provides a glimpse into the complex relationship between humans and animals in this ancient civilization.

To understand the significance of this discovery, we must delve into the role of cats in ancient Egyptian society. Cats were not merely pets; they were divine beings, associated with the goddess Bastet. This feline deity represented protection, fertility, and motherhood.

Egyptians mummified cats for various reasons; as offerings to Bastet, to accompany their owners into the afterlife and as a way to embody the goddess's protection.

The discovery at Beni Hassan was not just a cemetery; it was a treasure trove of cultural and religious significance, offering insights into ancient Egyptian beliefs and practices.

The fate of these mummified cats took an unexpected and controversial turn. In a decision that would horrify modern archaeologists and cat lovers alike, a significant portion of the mummies were shipped to Liverpool, England. Their destination? Not a museum or research facility, but farmers' fields.

In a twist of irony, these once revered feline remains were ground up and used as fertilizer. Estimates suggest that around 19 tonnes of cat mummies were used to enrich English soil, quite literally turning sacred history into growth for future harvests.

Alwy M. Jones

The Father of Algebra and Pioneer of Mathematics

Muhammad ibn Musa al-Khwarizmi, born around 780 CE in present day Uzbekistan and died around 850 CE, was a Persian polymath who made groundbreaking contributions to mathematics, astronomy, and geography. He is widely regarded as one of the most influential scholars of the Islamic Golden Age. Al-Khwarizmi's work laid the foundation for several branches of mathematics and had a profound impact on both Eastern and Western scientific thought for centuries to come.

Al-Khwarizmi is known as the "father of algebra" due to his seminal work in developing and systematizing this branch of mathematics. His most famous treatise, "Al-Kitab al-Mukhtasar fi Hisab al-Jabr wal-Muqabala" (The Compendious Book on Calculation by Completion and Balancing), introduced the fundamental concepts of algebra as a distinct discipline.

In this groundbreaking work, Al-Khwarizmi presented systematic solutions for linear and quadratic equations. He introduced the concept of reduction and balancing, which involves transposing terms from one side of an equation to the other. This method allowed for the solving of complex equations by simplifying them into standard forms.

The term "algebra" itself is derived from "al-jabr" in the title of his book, which refers to the process of moving terms to the other side of an equation. Al-Khwarizmi's work was translated into Latin in the 12th century, introducing algebra to the Western world and significantly influencing the development of mathematics in Europe.

The term "algorithm," which is ubiquitous in modern mathematics and computer science, is derived from Al-Khwarizmi's name. In his works, particularly on algebra and Indian numerals, Al-Khwarizmi described step by step procedures for solving mathematical problems. These systematic approaches to problem solving became known as algorithms.

An algorithm, in its simplest form, is a set of rules or procedures for solving a problem or performing a task. Al-Khwarizmi's methods for solving equations and performing arithmetic operations with Indian numerals were some of the earliest examples of algorithms in mathematics.

The concept of algorithms introduced by Al-Khwarizmi has had a far reaching impact, extending well beyond mathematics into the realm of computer science. Today, algorithms form the backbone of computer programming and are fundamental to the functioning of digital technologies.

Al-Khwarizmi played a crucial role in popularizing the Hindu-Arabic numeral system, which originated in India, throughout the Middle East and eventually Europe. His book "On the Calculation with Hindu Numerals," written around 825 CE, was instrumental in spreading the use of these numerals.

The Hindu-Arabic numeral system, which includes the digits 0 to 9, offered several advantages over previous numeral systems:

1. Simplicity: It used only ten symbols, making it easier to learn and use.

2. Positional notation: The value of a digit depends on its position, allowing for the representation of very large and very small numbers.

3. The concept of zero: This allowed for more accurate and diverse mathematical operations.

Al-Khwarizmi's work helped popularize this system, which eventually replaced the cumbersome Roman numeral system in Europe. The adoption of Hindu-Arabic numerals greatly facilitated mathematical calculations and scientific advancements.

Moreover, Al-Khwarizmi's promotion of the decimal system revolutionized mathematics. The decimal system, based on powers of 10, allowed for more efficient calculation methods and easier representation of fractions. This system became the foundation for modern arithmetic and greatly simplified mathematical operations in various fields, from commerce to scientific research.

Al-Khwarizmi's contributions to mathematics, particularly in algebra, algorithms, and the popularization of the Hindu-Arabic numeral system and decimal arithmetic, have had a lasting impact on the development of mathematics and science. His work bridges ancient mathematical traditions with modern practices, cementing his place as one of the most influential mathematicians in history.

Alwy M. Jones

Father of Modern Optics and Pioneer of the Scientific Method

Ibn al-Haytham, also known by his Latinized name Alhazen, was a pioneering Arab scientist who lived from 965 to 1040 CE. He made groundbreaking contributions to the fields of optics, mathematics, astronomy, and the development of the scientific method.

Ibn al-Haytham lived during the height of the Islamic Golden Age, a period of great scientific and cultural advancement in the Muslim world. This era was characterized by a flourishing of knowledge and scholarship, translation and preservation of ancient Greek and Roman texts and patronage of scientists and scholars by rulers.

Ibn al-Haytham was born in Basra (modern-day Iraq) but spent much of his working life in Cairo, Egypt. These cities were major centers of learning and scientific inquiry during his time.

Ibn al-Haytham's most famous work, the "Book of Optics," revolutionized the understanding of vision and light. Key concepts introduced in this book include rejection of the emission theory of vision, explanation of how the eye works and description of the camera obscura principle.

Ibn al-Haytham proposed that vision occurs when light reflects off an object and enters the eye, light travels in straight lines and the eye functions similarly to a pinhole camera.

He conducted extensive experiments on the reflection of light from various surfaces, the refraction of light through different media and the properties of lenses and mirrors.

Ibn al-Haytham stressed the importance of experimental evidence in scientific inquiry. He conducted systematic experiments to test hypotheses, used quantitative measurements and mathematical models and emphasized the need for repeatability in experiments.

He advocated for questioning established beliefs and authorities, seeking empirical evidence to support or refute theories and acknowledging and correcting errors in one's own work.

Roger Bacon (1214-1292) an English philosopher and scientist was greatly influenced by Ibn al-Haytham's work adopted Ibn al-Haytham's experimental approach, expanded on his ideas about optics and vision and introduce Ibn al-Haytham's ideas to medieval Europe.

Johannes Kepler (1571-1630) a German astronomer and mathematician built upon Ibn al-Haytham's optical theories; used Ibn al-Haytham's work as a foundation for his own studies on the nature of light, developed a more accurate model of vision based on Ibn al-Haytham's ideas and applied optical principles to the design of telescopes.

Ibn al-Haytham's work laid the foundation for the development of modern optics, the invention of optical instruments like telescopes and microscopes and our current understanding of how vision works.

His emphasis on experimentation and empirical evidence contributed to the development of the modern scientific method, a shift away from reliance on ancient authorities in scientific inquiry and the promotion of skepticism and critical thinking in research.

Ibn al-Haytham's approach influenced the relationship between theory and observation in science, ideas about the nature of scientific knowledge and its limitations and the role of mathematics in describing natural phenomena.

Alwy M. Jones

A Victorian Doctor's Daring Invention

In the annals of medical history, few inventions are as bizarre and potentially dangerous as the tapeworm trap devised by a Victorian doctor in the late 19th century. This peculiar device, designed to combat a common parasitic infection, showcases both the ingenuity and the risks associated with early medical innovations.

Dr. Theodore Bilharz, a German physician working in Egypt during the 1850s, is credited with inventing this unusual tapeworm trap. Bilharz, known for his work on parasitic diseases, sought a solution to the persistent problem of tapeworm infections, which were widespread in his time due to poor sanitation and inadequate food preparation practices.

Bilharz's invention was deceptively simple in design but audacious in concept. The trap consisted of a small metal cage, approximately the size of a large pill, attached to a long string. Inside the cage was a piece of food, typically a small morsel of meat, intended to lure the tapeworm. The patient would swallow the cage, which was closed but had small openings. The string attached to the cage would remain outside the patient's mouth. The trap would pass through the esophagus and into the stomach and intestines. The tapeworm, attracted by the bait, would enter the cage through the small openings. Once the tapeworm was inside, the doctor would quickly pull the string, retrieving the cage and the trapped parasite.

Alwy M. Jones

Ancient Wisdom in Emergency Medicine

The Maasai people of East Africa have long been known for their rich cultural traditions and unique practices. Among their lesser known but remarkable achievements is their early mastery of tracheotomy, a lifesaving surgical procedure that predates similar practices in Europe. This article explores the history, techniques, and significance of Maasai tracheotomy, shedding light on an often overlooked aspect of indigenous medical knowledge.

The Maasai are a Nilotic ethnic group inhabiting northern, central and southern Kenya and northern Tanzania. Their society is traditionally pastoral, with a strong warrior culture. The Maasai's medical practices, including tracheotomy, developed as part of their need to address emergencies in remote areas, far from modern medical facilities.

While precise dating of the origin of Maasai tracheotomy is challenging due to the oral nature of their historical records, anthropological evidence suggests the practice has existed for centuries, potentially predating similar techniques in Europe by a significant margin.

The Maasai tracheotomy procedure, known as "cutting the neck" in their language, involves creating an opening in the trachea to allow air to enter the lungs when the upper airway is obstructed. The procedure is typically performed in cases of severe throat swelling, often resulting from snake bites or other injuries.

The patient is positioned with the neck extended. The location for the incision is identified, usually between the cricoid cartilage and the sternal notch. A quick, precise incision is made through the skin and into the trachea. The hollow reed or bone is inserted to maintain an open airway. The wound is treated with honey and monitored for complications.

Alwy M. Jones

A Dark Chapter in History

Slave breeding, the systematic coercion of enslaved people into reproduction for economic gain, stands as a grotesque chapter in the annals of human history. This practice, rooted in the dehumanization of enslaved Africans, inflicted immeasurable suffering and had far reaching consequences.

The institution of slavery, particularly in the American South, provided the fertile ground for the development of slave breeding. The economic demands of plantation agriculture, coupled with the declining transatlantic slave trade, created a situation where breeding enslaved people became a profitable enterprise. While the concept of breeding humans for profit was not explicitly codified into law, it was a pervasive practice understood by slaveholders and enslaved people alike.

Figures like George Washington and Thomas Jefferson, despite their roles as Founding Fathers, owned enslaved people and participated in the system that perpetuated slave breeding. Their papers and correspondence offer glimpses into the cold calculations involved in this practice.

Slave breeding was a calculated and systematic process. Enslaved men and women were often paired based on perceived physical attributes, with the aim of producing strong, healthy offspring. Coercion, violence, and psychological manipulation were employed to ensure compliance.

The living conditions of enslaved people involved in breeding were often particularly harsh. Women were subjected to back breaking labor while pregnant, increasing the risk of complications and infant mortality. Children born into slavery faced a life of toil and subjugation, perpetuating the cycle of exploitation.

Slave breeding represents the ultimate violation of human dignity and rights. It reduced enslaved people to mere commodities, their bodies and reproductive capacities exploited for profit. The practice was rooted in a racist ideology that dehumanized Black people, justifying their enslavement and the horrific treatment they endured.

The psychological and emotional trauma inflicted on enslaved individuals through forced breeding is immeasurable. The practice shattered families, destroyed lives, and created a legacy of intergenerational trauma.

The children born from these forced unions grew up in a world of oppression and inequality. They inherited the legacy of their enslaved parents, facing a lifetime of discrimination and marginalization. The psychological and emotional scars of slave breeding have been passed down through generations, impacting the lives of Black people for centuries.

Alwy M. Jones

A Controversial Figure in World War II and Beyond

World War II marked one of the darkest periods in human history, with the rise of Nazism in Germany posing an unprecedented threat to global peace and human rights. The Nazi regime's aggressive expansion and racist ideology directly supported the principles of Christianity, creating a complex and dangerous environment for religious institutions across Europe.

Eugenio Pacelli, who would become Pope Pius XII, was born in Rome in 1876. He had a distinguished career in the Catholic Church, serving as nuncio (papal ambassador) to Germany from 1917 to 1929. This experience gave him firsthand knowledge of German politics and culture. Pacelli was elected pope in 1939, just months before the outbreak of World War II.

Pope Pius XII's actions during World War II have been the subject of intense debate and scrutiny. Critics argue that he failed to speak out forcefully against Nazi atrocities, particularly the Holocaust. They point to his Christmas message of 1942, which only vaguely alluded to the suffering of millions, without explicitly mentioning Jews or Nazis.

One of the most controversial aspects of Pope Pius XII's legacy involves allegations of his involvement in helping Nazi war criminals escape justice after the war. This network of escape routes, often referred to as the "ratlines," reportedly facilitated the movement of over 8,000 Nazis to countries such as Britain, Canada, Spain, America, and Argentina.

The escape of Adolf Eichmann, one of the main organizers of the Holocaust, to Argentina. Some argue that this was made possible through Church connected networks. The flight of Croatian war criminal Ante Pavelic, who allegedly received assistance from Catholic clergy. The case of Klaus Barbie, the "Butcher of Lyon," who escaped to Bolivia with alleged help from U.S. intelligence and Church affiliated individuals.

While direct evidence linking Pope Pius XII to these escapes remains contentious, the involvement of some Catholic clergy and institutions in assisting former Nazis is well documented.

Alwy M. Jones

Muslims in the British War Effort

The Second World War was a global conflict that mobilized entire nations. While the contributions of European and North American powers are well-documented, the role of Muslims in the British war effort often remains in the shadows. Over 50 million Muslims, hailing from diverse backgrounds and colonies, played a pivotal role in the fight against Nazi Germany and its allies.

The early 20th century witnessed the rise of Islamic resistance to colonial rule, yet many Muslim communities also found themselves caught in the maelstrom of World War II. The war presented a complex dilemma; while colonial powers were the oppressors, the enemy; Nazi Germany represented a far greater threat to global security and, in many cases, to Islamic lands themselves. This confluence of factors motivated many Muslims to join the fight against fascism. Muslim soldiers from across the British Empire served in various capacities. Indian, Pakistani, and Bangladeshi troops formed the backbone of the British Indian Army, which was instrumental in North Africa and Burma campaigns. Malayan troops fought bravely in the jungles of Southeast Asia. Beyond the battlefield, Muslims contributed significantly to the war effort. They served in support roles, such as medical corps, engineering, and logistics. In Britain itself, Muslim communities offered support to the war effort through fundraising, volunteering, and civil defense.

Intelligence gathering was another crucial area of Muslim contribution. The British Indian Army's intelligence units, comprising soldiers from diverse backgrounds, played a vital role in gathering information about Axis activities. This intelligence often proved invaluable in turning the tide of battle.

The contributions of Muslim soldiers were indispensable to the Allied victory. Their bravery and resilience in the face of adversity helped to turn the tide in crucial battles. For instance, the Indian Army's role in the North African campaign was pivotal in halting Rommel's advance.

Furthermore, the support provided by Muslim communities at home helped to sustain the war effort. By maintaining morale and contributing to the economy, they ensured that the war machine continued to function effectively.

The decision to join the war effort was not without its complexities. While many Muslims were motivated by a sense of duty and patriotism, others were influenced by religious beliefs that emphasized the defense of one's homeland and community. The war also presented an opportunity for Muslim soldiers to challenge colonial stereotypes and demonstrate their loyalty to the Crown.

However, the war experience was not without its challenges. Racial prejudice and discrimination were issues faced by many Muslim soldiers. Despite these obstacles, they persevered, their contributions a testament to their resilience and courage.

Alwy M. Jones

A Polymath of the Islamic Golden Age

Abu Rayhan al-Biruni, born in 973 CE in Kath, Khwarezm (modern-day Uzbekistan), was one of the most brilliant minds of the Islamic Golden Age. Growing up in a region known for its rich intellectual tradition, Al-Biruni received a comprehensive education in mathematics, astronomy, and other sciences. He lived during a time of great political turmoil but managed to thrive intellectually under various patrons, including Mahmud of Ghazni.

Al-Biruni's insatiable curiosity led him to master multiple languages, including Arabic, Persian, Sanskrit, and Greek, allowing him to access and synthesize knowledge from various cultures. His extensive travels, including a long stay in India, greatly influenced his work and broadened his perspectives.

Al-Biruni made significant contributions to mathematics, particularly in the fields of trigonometry and geometry. He developed new methods for solving complex mathematical problems, including techniques for calculating the radius of the Earth. Al-Biruni introduced the concept of specific gravity and created precise tables for calculating it. He made advancements in spherical trigonometry, which were crucial for his astronomical work. Al-Biruni also worked on solving cubic equations and contributed to the development of algebra.

In astronomy, Al-Biruni's work was groundbreaking. He calculated the Earth's radius with remarkable accuracy, arriving at a figure of 6,339.6 km, which is only 16.8 km less than the modern value. Al-Biruni invented new instruments for astronomical observations, including an improved astrolabe. He accurately determined the latitudes and longitudes of many places, enhancing geographical knowledge and navigation. Al-Biruni also made detailed observations of solar and lunar eclipses, contributing to a better understanding of celestial mechanics.

Al-Biruni's contributions to geography were equally impressive. He authored "Kitab al-Hind" (The Book of India), a comprehensive study of Indian geography, customs, and sciences, which remains a valuable historical source. Al-Biruni developed methods for determining the direction of Mecca from any point on Earth, crucial for Islamic religious practices. He proposed the existence of a landmass in the southern hemisphere, anticipating the discovery of the Americas. Al-Biruni's work in cartography improved the accuracy of world maps of his time.

One of Al-Biruni's most forward thinking contributions was his discussion on the possibility of Earth's rotation. He presented arguments both for and against the Earth's rotation around its axis, showing a remarkably open-minded approach to scientific inquiry. Al-Biruni suggested that if the Earth rotated, it would not affect the apparent motions of celestial bodies, an idea far ahead of his time. While he did not definitively conclude that the Earth rotates, his willingness to consider the possibility challenged the prevailing Ptolemaic model and laid groundwork for future astronomers.

Al-Biruni's impact on science and scholarship has been profound and long-lasting. His methodical approach to scientific inquiry, emphasizing observation and experimentation, helped pave the way for the modern scientific method. Al-Biruni's work in mathematics, especially his advancements in trigonometry, influenced later mathematicians and astronomers. His accurate calculations of the Earth's radius and other geographical data improved navigation and cartography for centuries. Al-Biruni's open-mindedness and cross-cultural approach to knowledge set an example for future scholars, promoting a more inclusive and comprehensive view of science. His writings, preserved and translated over the centuries, continue to provide valuable insights into the scientific knowledge and methodologies of the Islamic Golden Age.

Al-Biruni stands as one of the greatest polymaths in history. His contributions spanned multiple disciplines and his innovative approaches to scientific problems laid the groundwork for future advancements. Al-Biruni's legacy is not just in the specific discoveries he made, but in the spirit of inquiry, cross-cultural understanding, and methodical research that he exemplified, inspiring generations of scientists and scholars across various fields.

Alwy M. Jones

Yemen's Hidden Legacy

Coffee, one of the world's most beloved beverages, has a rich and complex history that is often misunderstood. While many believe that coffee originated in Ethiopia, compelling evidence suggests that Yemen is the true birthplace of coffee as we know it today.

Coffee cultivation in Yemen dates back to at least the 15th century. The first credible evidence of coffee drinking appears in the Sufi monasteries of Yemen around 1450 CE. Yemeni Sufi monk Ali ibn Omar al-Shadhili is credited with discovering coffee's stimulating effects and introducing its consumption as a beverage.

Key historical events include:

- 1450 - 1470 CE: Coffee drinking becomes widespread in Yemeni Sufi circles.

- 1511 CE: The first coffee houses open in Mecca, sparking controversy and temporary bans.

- 16th century: Coffee cultivation expands in Yemen, particularly in the region of Mocha.

Coffee holds immense cultural importance in Yemen. Traditional Yemeni coffee, known as qahwa, is prepared using a method distinct from modern brewing techniques. The beans are lightly roasted and ground with cardamom and sometimes other spices. This preparation is central to social gatherings and hospitality rituals.

Yemeni coffee culture emphasizes the communal aspect of coffee drinking. It's common for people to gather in the afternoon for qat chewing sessions, where coffee is served as a complementary beverage.

The belief that Ethiopia is coffee's birthplace stems from legends about a goatherd named Kaldi discovering coffee's energizing effects on his goats. While wild coffee plants (Coffea arabica) are indeed native to Ethiopia, there's no historical evidence of coffee being consumed as a beverage there before its cultivation in Yemen.

Yemen's claim to being coffee's true origin is supported by first documented evidence of coffee drinking, development of coffee roasting and brewing methods and the establishment of the first coffee trade.

Yemen's port of Mocha became the center of the global coffee trade in the 16th and 17th centuries. From here, coffee spread to Egypt and the Ottoman Empire (late 16th century), Europe (early 17th century) and India and Southeast Asia (mid-17th century).

Yemeni authorities maintained a monopoly on coffee production by prohibiting the export of fertile beans, ensuring all coffee traded came through Yemen.

Alwy M. Jones

The Prince of Physicians

Ibn Sina, known in the West as Avicenna, was a Persian polymath who lived from 980 to 1037 CE. He is widely regarded as one of the most influential thinkers and medical scholars of the Islamic Golden Age.

Ibn Sina lived during a period of great intellectual ferment in the Islamic world. The Abbasid Caliphate, though politically in decline, still fostered a rich culture of learning and scientific inquiry. This era saw the translation and preservation of Greek, Roman, and Persian texts, which formed the basis for further advancements in various fields. Born in 980 CE near Bukhara (in present-day Uzbekistan), Ibn Sina showed early signs of exceptional intellect. By the age of 10, he had memorized the Quran and by 18, he had mastered logic, natural sciences, and medicine. His voracious appetite for knowledge led him to study the works of Greek philosophers and physicians, particularly those of Aristotle and Galen.

Ibn Sina's magnum opus, "Al-Qanun fi al-Tibb" (The Canon of Medicine), was a comprehensive medical encyclopedia that synthesized Greek, Arab, and Persian medical knowledge with his own observations and experiments. The Canon was divided into five books; General Principles of Medicine, Materia Medica, Diseases Affecting Particular Organs, Diseases Affecting the Whole Body and Compound Drugs.

The Canon introduced several innovative concepts, emphasis on experimentation and clinical observation, recognition of the contagious nature of certain diseases, introduction of quarantine for infectious diseases and detailed descriptions of over 760 drugs. The Canon was translated into Latin in the 12th century and became the standard medical text in European universities until the 17th century. Its influence on Western medicine was profound and long lasting. Ibn Sina made significant contributions to Islamic philosophy, particularly in metaphysics and logic. His work "Kitab al-Shifa" (The Book of Healing) was a comprehensive philosophical and scientific encyclopedia.

In astronomy, Ibn Sina made observations on stars and planets, and proposed an instrument for observing the coordinates of stars, which was a precursor to the telescope.

Ibn Sina's work in chemistry included studies on the properties of metals and minerals. He also described the process of distillation and the production of essential oils.

Ibn Sina's contributions to medicine and science had a lasting impact, his medical theories and practices influenced European medicine for centuries. His philosophical works played a crucial role in the transmission of Aristotelian thought to the West. His emphasis on empirical observation and experimentation contributed to the development of the scientific method.

Alwy M. Jones

Pioneering Surgical Techniques and Anatomical Knowledge

The civilization of ancient Egypt, renowned for its monumental architecture and intricate burial practices, was also home to a sophisticated medical tradition that included advanced surgical procedures and a nuanced understanding of human anatomy.

The ancient Egyptians' knowledge of human anatomy was far more advanced than previously believed. This understanding was primarily derived from the practice of mummification, which involved removing and preserving internal organs, provided Egyptian embalmers and physicians with extensive knowledge of human anatomy. Ancient Egyptian medical texts, such as the Edwin Smith Papyrus and the Ebers Papyrus, contain detailed descriptions of various anatomical structures and their functions.

These sources of knowledge allowed Egyptian physicians to develop a sophisticated understanding of the human body, which in turn enabled them to perform complex surgical procedures.

One of the most impressive surgical procedures performed by ancient Egyptian physicians was cataract removal. This delicate operation demonstrates their advanced understanding of ocular anatomy and surgical techniques.

Egyptian physicians used a variety of specialized tools, including bronze scalpels, forceps, and needles. The primary method for cataract removal involved using a needle to push the cloudy lens of the eye downward, out of the field of vision. This technique, known as "couching," was remarkably effective for its time. Egyptian physicians used honey, wine, and other natural substances as antiseptics to prevent infection. Various herbal remedies and possibly hypnosis were employed to manage pain during and after surgery.

The ability to perform such a delicate procedure speaks to the high level of skill and knowledge possessed by ancient Egyptian surgeons. It's important to note that while this technique was not as advanced as modern cataract surgery, it was a significant achievement for its time and often resulted in improved vision for patients.

In addition to cataract surgery, ancient Egyptian physicians were capable of performing a range of other complex procedures like;

1. Trepanation: The practice of drilling holes in the skull to relieve pressure or treat head injuries.

2. Dental surgery: Evidence suggests they performed tooth extractions and even attempted to treat abscesses.

3. Trauma surgery: The Edwin Smith Papyrus contains detailed instructions for treating various wounds and fractures.

Halima Cisse

In May 2021, the world watched in awe as Halima Cisse, a 27 year old woman from Mali, defied all odds by giving birth to nine healthy babies; nonuplets, naturally. This remarkable event not only shattered medical records but also shone a light on the strength and resilience of mothers around the globe. Halima, before this extraordinary pregnancy, lived a relatively private life. Information regarding her health prior to the nonuplet conception is limited. However, childbirth in Mali carries its own set of challenges. Access to specialized medical care, particularly in rural areas, can be limited.

Halima's story unfolded in the Ain Borja clinic in Casablanca, Morocco. Due to the complexity of the pregnancy and the increased risk associated with carrying nine babies, Halima was transferred there for closer medical monitoring. The birth itself, on May 5th 2021, was a marvel of nature. Halima defied medical expectations by delivering the nonuplets through cesarean section.

The nine babies; five girls and four boys were born prematurely. Despite their early arrival, all the nonuplets were reported to be in "perfect health" according to medical personnel following their birth. However, the challenges of caring for nine newborns simultaneously were immense. The babies required specialized care in an incubator for an extended period.

Alwy M. Jones

The "Great White Hope"

James J. Jeffries, known as the "Boilermaker," was a heavyweight boxing champion whose 1910 comeback attempt against Jack Johnson became a pivotal moment in American sports and race relations.

Born in 1875 in Ohio, Jeffries began his professional boxing career in 1896. He quickly rose through the ranks, becoming the world heavyweight champion in 1899 by defeating Bob Fitzsimmons. Jeffries successfully defended his title multiple times before retiring undefeated in 1905.

In 1908, Jack Johnson became the first African American heavyweight champion, defeating Tommy Burns. Johnson's victory and flamboyant lifestyle outside the ring challenged prevailing racial attitudes in the United States.

Jeffries' return to boxing in 1910 was framed as a quest to reclaim the title for the white race. He was dubbed the "Great White Hope," a term that encapsulated the racial tensions of the era. Many white Americans, uncomfortable with Johnson's success and public persona, saw Jeffries as their champion to reassert perceived racial superiority.

The bout between Jeffries and Johnson, held on July 4th 1910, in Reno, Nevada, was billed as "The Fight of the Century." It attracted enormous attention, with racial undertones dominating the pre-fight narrative. Jeffries, who had been retired for five years, trained intensively to regain his form.

Johnson decisively defeated Jeffries, who was knocked down multiple times before his corner threw in the towel in the 15th round. The result sent shockwaves through American society. In several cities, Johnson's victory sparked racial violence, with white mobs attacking African Americans in retaliation.

The fight's outcome challenged deeply held racial beliefs about white physical superiority. It forced many to confront their prejudices and the reality of African American achievement in a highly visible arena. The event highlighted how sports could become a battleground for larger social and racial issues.

Alwy M. Jones

The Brutal Murder of James Byrd Jr

James Byrd Jr. was a 49 year old African American man born and raised in Jasper, Texas. A father of three, Byrd was known in his community as a friendly, easygoing person who enjoyed singing in his church choir. His life was tragically cut short in a horrific act of racial violence that shocked the nation.

The late 1990s in the United States were marked by persistent racial tensions, despite progress in civil rights. While overt racism had become less socially acceptable, underlying prejudices and systemic inequalities remained prevalent, particularly in some southern states with histories of racial conflict.

On June 7th 1998, in Jasper, Texas, Byrd was walking home when he was offered a ride by three white men; Shawn Berry, Lawrence Russell Brewer, and John William King. Instead of taking him home, the men drove Byrd to a secluded area where they severely beat him, urinated on him, and chained him by his ankles to the back of their pickup truck.

They then drove for approximately 3 miles, dragging Byrd's body along an asphalt road. The ordeal ended when Byrd's body hit a culvert, severing his right arm and head. The killers dumped his remains in front of an African-American cemetery and went to a barbecue.

The three perpetrators had diverse but troubling backgrounds. King and Brewer were avowed white supremacists who had joined racist prison gangs. Berry, while not explicitly tied to white supremacist groups, associated with King and Brewer.

The crime was immediately recognized as racially motivated. King and Brewer's involvement in white supremacist organizations, coupled with racist tattoos and paraphernalia found in their possession, clearly indicated their hatred toward African Americans. The brutality of the crime and the specific targeting of Byrd due to his race led to its classification as a hate crime.

This classification was significant as it allowed for harsher sentencing and brought national attention to the need for comprehensive hate crime legislation. The incident became a stark reminder that violent racism was still a present danger in American society.

All three men were tried separately. John William King was found guilty of capital murder and sentenced to death in February 1999. Lawrence Russell Brewer was also convicted of capital murder and sentenced to death in September 1999. Shawn Berry, who cooperated with authorities, was spared the death penalty but received a life sentence in November 1999.

Brewer was executed by lethal injection on September 21st 2011. King was executed on April 24th 2019, after numerous appeals. Berry remains in prison, eligible for parole in 2038.

Alwy M. Jones

Chinese Workers in Israel

Since the 1990s, Israel has relied on foreign workers, including a significant number from China, to fill labor shortages in various sectors. Chinese workers primarily occupy positions in construction, agriculture, and caregiving. This influx of foreign labor has been driven by Israel's economic growth and demographic challenges, as well as the desire to reduce dependence on Palestinian workers following periods of conflict.

Recent reports have highlighted a troubling clause in some employment contracts for Chinese workers in Israel. This clause explicitly prohibits these workers from engaging in sexual relations with Israeli Jews. The exact wording varies, but typically states that workers agree not to "form intimate relationships" or "have any sexual contact" with Israeli citizens, specifically mentioning Jews.

Such clauses raise serious ethical concerns, infringing on personal freedoms and potentially violating human rights. They also reflect problematic assumptions about race, nationality, and sexuality. Legal experts question the enforceability of such provisions, as they likely contravene basic principles of individual liberty and non-discrimination.

These contractual stipulations are symptomatic of broader issues of racism and discrimination in Israeli society. Sociologists argue that such practices reinforce existing racial hierarchies and perpetuate harmful stereotypes about foreign workers. These clauses reflect deep seated fears about racial 'purity' and demonstrate how foreign workers are often dehumanized and seen solely as economic units rather than individuals with rights and personal lives.

Human rights activists point out that these contracts contribute to the marginalization of foreign workers, creating an environment where they are treated as second-class residents. This approach contradicts principles of equality and respect for human dignity.

Alwy M. Jones

The Golden Trade of the Moors and Mali

The possibility that African merchants, particularly those from the Mali Empire and Moorish traders, reached the Americas before Christopher Columbus has been a subject of debate among historians and researchers for decades.

The Mali Empire (c. 1235-1670) was one of the largest and wealthiest empires in West Africa during the middle Ages. At its peak, it covered an area larger than Western Europe and was renowned for its wealth in gold and salt. The empire's most famous ruler, Mansa Musa (reigned 1312-1337), was known for his extravagant pilgrimage to Mecca, which showcased Mali's immense wealth and sophisticated trade networks.

The Moors, a term historically applied to the Muslim inhabitants of the Maghreb, southern Iberia, Sicily, and Malta, were also prolific traders during this period. Their maritime expertise and extensive trade networks stretched across the Mediterranean and along the West African coast.

The primary trade routes of the Mali Empire and Moorish merchants were; Trans-Saharan trade routes; connecting West Africa to North Africa and the Mediterranean. West African coastal routes; Along the Atlantic coast of Africa. Mediterranean Sea routes; Linking North Africa to Europe and the Middle East. These routes facilitated the exchange of gold, salt, ivory, textiles, and slaves, contributing significantly to the economic prosperity of West Africa and the Mediterranean region.

Several historians and researchers have proposed that Malian and Moorish traders may have reached the Americas before Columbus.

According to 14th century Malian historian Al-Umari, Abu Bakr II, predecessor of Mansa Musa, abdicated his throne to lead an expedition of 2,000 ships into the Atlantic Ocean in search of the limits of the sea. Some researchers speculate that this expedition may have reached the Americas.

Some scholars point to similarities between certain Native American and West African languages, as well as cultural practices, as potential evidence of pre-Columbian contact.

The presence of crops native to Africa, such as cotton and banana plants, in pre-Columbian American contexts has been cited as possible evidence of early African voyages.

Some researchers interpret certain artifacts found in the Americas, such as the Olmec heads in Mexico, as having African features, suggesting possible early contact.

Alwy M. Jones

The Father of Modern Surgery

Abu al-Qasim Khalaf ibn al-Abbas al-Zahrawi, known in the West as Abulcasis, was a pioneering Arab Muslim physician, surgeon, and chemist who lived from 936 to 1013 CE. Widely regarded as the father of modern surgery, Al-Zahrawi made significant contributions to the field of medicine, particularly through his monumental work "Al-Tasrif."

Al-Zahrawi lived during the height of the Islamic Golden Age in Al-Andalus (Muslim ruled Spain). This period was characterized by great advancements in science, medicine, and philosophy. Cordoba, where Al-Zahrawi spent most of his life, was a center of learning and cultural exchange between Islamic, Christian, and Jewish scholars.

"Kitab al-Tasrif" (The Method of Medicine) was Al-Zahrawi's magnum opus, a 30 volume medical encyclopedia that covered a wide range of medical topics. It was the result of almost 50 years of medical practice and observations.

The encyclopedia covered various aspects of medicine, including; general medical principles, pharmacology, therapeutics, surgical procedures and instruments, ophthalmology and obstetrics and gynecology.

"Al-Tasrif" was translated into Latin in the 12th century and became a standard medical text in European universities for centuries. It was the first illustrated work on surgery and surgical instruments, providing detailed descriptions and drawings that were unprecedented for its time.

Al-Zahrawi described over 200 surgical instruments, many of which he invented himself. He introduced techniques for treating bone fractures, methods for reducing dislocations, procedures for removing kidney stones and techniques for dental surgery and extraction.

Some of Al-Zahrawi's groundbreaking techniques included the use of catgut for internal stitching (which is still in use today), the use of forceps in obstetrics, the cauterization of wounds and ligature of blood vessels before amputation.

Al-Zahrawi invented numerous surgical instruments, including; scalpels, bone saws, forceps, specula and surgical needles.

Alwy M. Jones

The Raising of Italy's Minimum Marriage Age

In 1892, Italy took a significant step in addressing child marriage by raising the minimum age for marriage for girls to 12 years old. This decision, while shocking by modern standards, represented a progressive move for its time and laid the groundwork for future reforms.

In late 19th century Italy, as in much of Europe, child marriage was not uncommon, particularly in rural areas and among the lower classes. The practice was deeply rooted in traditions that viewed marriage as an economic and social contract between families rather than a union based on love or personal choice.

Prior to 1892, there was no uniform minimum age for marriage in Italy. Local customs and religious laws often governed marital practices, leading to significant variations across regions. In some areas, girls as young as 7 or 8 were betrothed or married, though consummation typically occurred later.

Following the unification of Italy in 1861, there was a push to standardize laws across the country and align with more progressive European nations. Medical professionals raised awareness about the physical and psychological harm of early marriage and childbearing on young girls. There was a growing recognition of the importance of education for girls, which was hindered by early marriage.

Italy faced criticism from other European nations for its lack of protections for young girls. Early feminist groups in Italy advocated for women's rights, including protection from child marriage.

The decision to set the minimum age at 12 was a compromise between progressive reformers and conservative elements in Italian society. The Catholic Church, which held significant sway in Italy, traditionally recognized puberty as the appropriate age for marriage. In poor families, marrying off daughters early was seen as a way to reduce financial burden. Many Italians viewed early marriage as a means of preserving family honor and ensuring girls' chastity. The diverse cultures within Italy meant that marriage practices varied significantly across regions.

Alwy M. Jones

Pioneer of Chemistry and Alchemy

Jabir ibn Hayyan, known in the West as Geber, was a prominent Muslim polymath who lived approximately between 721 and 815 CE. Born in Tus, Khorasan (in present day Iran), Jabir grew up during the early years of the Abbasid Caliphate, a period marked by significant scientific and cultural advancements.

Jabir received a comprehensive education, studying under the Imam Ja'far al-Sadiq, which exposed him to various fields of knowledge. He later served as a court alchemist and physician to the Abbasid Caliph Harun al-Rashid.

During the Islamic Golden Age, Jabir played a crucial role in the development of chemistry and alchemy. He bridged the gap between ancient alchemical practices and the emergence of chemistry as a scientific discipline. His work laid the foundation for the systematic study of chemical substances and reactions.

Jabir ibn Hayyan made numerous significant contributions to the fields of chemistry and alchemy. Jabir refined and documented the process of crystallization, which is fundamental in purifying and isolating chemical compounds. He improved distillation techniques, developing more efficient apparatus for the separation of liquids based on their boiling points. Jabir described the process of sublimation, where a solid transforms directly into a gas without passing through the liquid state.

Jabir is credited with the discovery or improved production of citric acid, acetic acid, tartaric acid, arsenic and antimony from their sulfides.

He invented or improved various pieces of laboratory equipment, such as the alembic still, which became a standard tool in chemical laboratories for centuries.

Jabir developed a systematic classification of chemical substances, categorizing them based on their properties and reactions.

He proposed early theories of chemical combination and the nature of metals, which, while not entirely accurate, laid groundwork for future scientific inquiry.

Jabir authored numerous works, collectively known as the "Jabirian corpus."

- "Kitab al-Kimya" (The Book of Chemistry)

- "Kitab al-Sab'een" (The Book of Seventy)

- "Kitab al-Mizan" (The Book of the Balance)

These texts were widely circulated and translated, influencing both Islamic and Western alchemists and chemists for centuries.

Jabir emphasized the importance of systematic experimentation and accurate observation, contributing to the development of the scientific method in chemistry.

His work influenced many later scientists, including Al-Razi, Avicenna, and even European alchemists during the middle Ages and Renaissance.

The distillation and crystallization techniques he refined are still fundamental in various industrial chemical processes, including oil refining and pharmaceutical production.

Basic laboratory procedures such as filtration, evaporation, and melting, which Jabir systematized, remain essential in modern chemical research and education.

Jabir's work on the extraction and purification of natural substances laid the groundwork for modern pharmaceutical chemistry.

His theories on the nature of metals and their transformations influenced the development of modern materials science and metallurgy.

Alwy M. Jones

Polymath of the Islamic Golden Age

Omar Khayyam was born in 1048 CE in Nishapur, Iran, during the Seljuk Empire era. He lived during a time of great intellectual and cultural flourishing known as the Islamic Golden Age. Khayyam received a comprehensive education in mathematics, astronomy, and philosophy under notable scholars of his time, including Imam Muwaffaq Nishaburi.

Khayyam's life spanned a period of political turbulence, but he managed to gain patronage from various rulers, allowing him to pursue his scholarly interests. He spent significant time in Samarkand and Isfahan, two major centers of learning in the medieval Islamic world.

One of Khayyam's most significant contributions to mathematics was his work on cubic equations. He developed a geometric method for solving cubic equations by intersecting conic sections. This approach was revolutionary for its time and laid the groundwork for algebraic geometry.

Key achievements in this area include:

- Classification of all types of cubic equations

- Systematic solution methods for different cases

- Use of geometric constructions to solve algebraic problems

Khayyam made important contributions to the understanding of Euclid's parallel postulate. He attempted to prove the postulate using other axioms, and while unsuccessful, his work was crucial in the development of non-Euclidean geometry centuries later.

His approach included:

- Proposing alternative axioms

- Exploring the logical consequences of different geometric systems

- Laying the foundation for later developments in hyperbolic geometry

As an astronomer, Khayyam made several significant contributions he improved astronomical tables for calculating planetary positions, proposed a heliocentric theory, suggesting that the Earth rotates on its axis and made accurate observations of celestial phenomena.

Khayyam played a crucial role in reforming the Persian calendar. The resulting Jalali calendar, introduced in 1079 CE, was remarkably accurate for its time. Its key features included:

- A solar year of 365.24219858156 days, very close to the modern measurement

- Intercalation system more accurate than the Gregorian calendar

- Alignment with astronomical events and seasons

Khayyam is perhaps best known in the West for his poetry, particularly the collection of quatrains known as the Rubaiyat. These poems were popularized in the English-speaking world through Edward FitzGerald's translations in the 19th century.

Alwy M. Jones

The Case for Increasing Britain's Minimum Marriage Age

Historically, the age of marriage in Britain has been a contentious issue. In the 18th century, the renowned English jurist William Blackstone commented on the matter in his influential work "Commentaries on the Laws of England." Blackstone noted that the age of consent for marriage was 12 for girls and 14 for boys, though he expressed concerns about the maturity of individuals at these ages to enter into such a significant contract.

Blackstone wrote: "The law supposes them to be capable of contracting a valid marriage, as they are of other contracts... and so many sad consequences would follow if such contracts were absolutely void, that the law has thought proper to give them some validity."

While Blackstone's view reflected the norms of his time, it's clear that society has evolved significantly since then. The current minimum age for marriage in England, Wales, and Northern Ireland is 16 with parental consent, and 18 without parental consent. In Scotland, the minimum age is 16 with no parental consent required.

The Most Contradicting Book in Human History

According to Jewish culture the male child is circumcised within a few days of being born making it impossible to find an uncircumcised Jewish teenager let alone an adult.

In the book of Acts Chapter 15 verse 1 to 5 we find Paul (who was an adult) makes an argument against circumcision and through deductive reasoning proves that Paul who was an adult at the time was NOT circumcised; why would he make an argument against circumcision if he himself had upheld the covenant and had performed the tradition of circumcision.

This is proof beyond reasonable doubt that Paul was in fact NOT Jewish and by default NOT one of the disciples. The question now is who was Paul who was not Jewish nor a disciple and was responsible for writing a significant portion of the Bible? Are the speculations that he was a Roman infiltrator true? If he succeeded in contributing such a huge portion of the Bible, is the Bible in its entirety reliable as a result of the corruption by Paul? Further proof of Paul not upholding the covenant and Jewish tradition is exhibited in Galatians 5: 1-6. Coincidentally Galatians is among the Books said to have been written by Paul and is the same place where Jesus PBUH is referred to as a CURSE (Galatians 3:13). Clearly Paul dislikes Jesus PBUH.

Acts 15: 1-5 -> **1** certain people came down from Judea to Antioch and were teaching the believers: "Unless you are circumcised, according to the custom taught by Moses, you cannot be saved." **2** This brought Paul and Barnabas into sharp dispute and debate with them. So Paul and Barnabas were appointed, along with some other believers, to go up to Jerusalem to see the apostles and elders about this question. **3** The church sent them on their way, and as they traveled through Phoenicia and Samaria, they told how the Gentiles had been converted. This news made all the believers very glad. **4** When they came to Jerusalem, they were welcomed by the church and the apostles and elders, to whom they reported everything God had done through them. **5** Then some of the believers who belonged to the party of the Pharisees stood up and said, "The Gentiles must be circumcised and required to keep the Law of Moses."

Galatians 5: 1-6 -> **1** it is for freedom that Christ has set us free. Stand firm, then, and do not let yourselves be burdened again by a yoke of slavery. **2** Mark my words! I, Paul, tell you that if you let yourselves be circumcised, Christ will be of no value to you at all. **3** Again I declare to every man who lets himself be circumcised that he is obligated to obey the whole law. **4** You who are trying to be justified by the law have been alienated from Christ; you have fallen away from grace. **5** For through the Spirit we eagerly await by faith the righteousness for which we hope. **6** For in Christ Jesus neither circumcision nor uncircumcision has any value. The only thing that counts is faith expressing itself through love.

Galatians 3:13 -> **13** Christ redeemed us from the curse of the law by becoming a curse for us, for it is written: "Cursed is everyone who is hung on a pole.

Religious hypocrisy, defined as the practice of claiming to have moral standards or beliefs to which one's own behavior does not conform, has been a point of contention in Christianity, this often manifests as selective adherence to biblical laws, where certain scriptural teachings are emphasized while others are downplayed or ignored.

The 2024 Olympics held in France is one example where the Hypocrisy of Christianity is more so evident in their response when asked why they are not defending Jesus PBUH after he was supposedly mocked in the opening ceremony, to which they quote;

Matthew 5: 43 – 45 - "You have heard that it was said, 'Love your neighbor and hate your enemy.' But I tell you, love your enemies and pray for those who persecute you, that you may be children of your Father in heaven. He causes his sun to rise on the evil and the good, and sends rain on the righteous and the unrighteous.

Which is a direct contradiction to;

Luke 14 : 26 - "If anyone comes to me and does not hate father and mother, wife and children, brothers and sisters, yes, even their own life, such a person cannot be my disciple.

Favorite Verses Christians like to quote;

- Teachings on divorce (Matthew 19:9)

- Tithing (Malachi 3:10)

- Forgiveness (Matthew 5: 43 – 44)

Frequently Ignored or Reinterpreted Laws:

- Dietary restrictions (Leviticus 11)

- Prohibitions on wearing mixed fabrics (Leviticus 19:19)

- Instructions on slavery (Ephesians 6:5-9) (Leviticus 25: 44 – 46)

- Violence against women (25: 11 – 12)

- Tattoos (Leviticus 19:28)

- Interest (Deuteronomy 23:19) (Exodus 22:25)

- Hijab (1 Corinthians 11:5)

- Circumcision (Luke 2:21) (Genesis 17: 10 – 17)

- Violence (Joshua 10:40) (Deuteronomy 20:16) (Luke 19:27) (1 Samuel 15:3) (Numbers 31: 17 – 18)

- Just a Man (Matthew 21:11) (John 8: 39-40) (1 Timothy 2:5) (Remember Christians if you quote verses that claim Jesus PBUH is "God" you confirm that the Bible is a contradictory book. The EXACT definition of a contradictory book is when verse/sentence in a particular page says something the a verse/sentence in another page says something totally opposite what was said previously)

• <u>Galatians 3:10</u> - For all who rely on the works of the law are under a curse, as it is written: "Cursed is everyone who does not continue to do everything written in the Book of the Law.

Most Outstanding Contradiction

<u>John 8:14 - 14</u> - Jesus answered, "Even if I testify on my own behalf, my testimony is valid, for I know where I came from and where I am going. But you have no idea where I come from or where I am going.

<u>John 5:31</u> - "If I testify about myself, my testimony is not true.

But in spectacular fashion Christians would try to ignore the Old Testament trying to insinuate that they don't abide by it and that the New Testament is the new law in response choosing to suffer from selective amnesia forgetting that according to their doctrine Jesus PBUH is "God" and that the "Father" and "Son" are one therefore the commands that were given in the Old Testament are from Jesus PBUH (according to Christianity). By trying to make this argument Christians end up portraying their "God" as a confused being who issues laws and realize he made a mistake and tries to correct them by contradicting himself.

John 7:15-18 -> **15** The Jews there were amazed and asked, "How did this man get such learning without having been taught?" **16** Jesus answered, "My teaching is not my own. It comes from the one who SENT ME. **17** Anyone who chooses to do the will of God will find out whether my teaching comes from God or whether I speak on my own. **18** Whoever speaks on their own does so to gain personal glory, but he who seeks the glory of the one who sent him is a man of truth; there is nothing false about him.

Alwy M. Jones

The Significance of Age 12 in Jewish Culture

In Jewish culture, the age of 12 marks a pivotal milestone in a young person's life, signifying the transition from childhood to adulthood in religious terms.

The importance of age 12 in Jewish tradition can be traced back to ancient times. The Mishnah, a foundational text of rabbinic Judaism compiled around 200 CE, states that at 13, a boy becomes obligated to fulfill the commandments (Pirkei Avot 5:21). For girls, some sources indicate that this transition occurred at 12.

The age of 12 gained significance based on the understanding that it marked the onset of puberty and the development of moral reasoning. The Talmud (Niddah 45b) discusses physical and intellectual maturity signs, associating them with the ability to make vows and be held accountable for one's actions.

Bar Mitzvah (for boys) and Bat Mitzvah (for girls) are the ceremonies marking this transition to religious adulthood.

Traditionally occurring at age 13, this ceremony involves the boy being called to read from the Torah for the first time. The term "Bar Mitzvah" literally means "son of the commandment."

Bat Mitzvah: This ceremony for girls, typically at age 12, is a more recent development. It gained popularity in the 20th century, particularly in non-Orthodox communities. The term means "daughter of the commandment."

The individual becomes responsible for their actions under Jewish law. They are now obligated to follow all 613 commandments in the Torah. In traditional communities, males can now be counted in the quorum of ten required for certain prayers.

Alwy M. Jones

Women's Rights in Islamic and Christian Societies

The early Islamic period saw significant advancements in women's rights compared to pre-Islamic Arabian society. The Quran and teachings of Prophet Muhammad (SAW) introduced reforms that granted women legal rights and protections previously unavailable to them.

Key developments included:

- The right to inherit and own property

- The right to consent to marriage

- The right to education

- The right to participate in religious and social life

Notable female figures from early Islamic history include Khadijah (RA), Prophet Muhammad's(SAW) first wife and a successful businesswoman; Aisha (RA), a respected scholar and political leader; and Fatima al-Fihri, founder of the world's oldest university.

Islamic legal texts like the Quran and Hadith contained provisions supporting women's rights. For example, Surah An-Nisa in the Quran outlines inheritance rights for women, while numerous Hadiths encourage educating women.

In contrast, women in medieval Christian Europe (5th-15th centuries) and colonial America generally had fewer legal rights and protections:

- Most women could not own property or inherit in their own name

- Women had little say in marriage arrangements

- Access to formal education was extremely limited

- Participation in public life and leadership roles was restricted

The legal doctrine of coverture in England and America subsumed a woman's legal rights under those of her husband upon marriage. This persisted well into the 19th century in many Western nations.

Throughout Islamic history, women made significant contributions in various fields:

- Lubna of Cordoba (10th century): Mathematician and royal secretary in Spain

- Sitt al-Mulk (11th century): De facto ruler of the Fatimid Empire

- Razia Sultana (13th century): Ruler of the Delhi Sultanate

- Halide Edib Adıvar (20th century): Novelist, political leader and women's rights activist

A nuanced examination of history reveals that women's rights in Islamic societies were in many ways more advanced than those in Christian Europe and America for significant periods. However, the trajectory of these rights has varied greatly across different regions and time periods, influenced by a complex interplay of religious interpretation, cultural norms, and socio-political factors. Understanding this historical context is crucial for addressing contemporary challenges and fostering progress in women's rights across all societies.

Alwy M. Jones

MUHAMMAD (SAW) MARRIAGES

Muhammad's first marriage, to the wealthy businesswoman Khadija, lasted almost a quarter of a century and was monogamous throughout. The sources imply that theirs was a true love match in a society where marriage was an issue more of socio-political expediency than of romance and the emotions.

His second wife, Sawda, was an early convert to Islam and the widow of one of his close followers. Subsequent to the Hijra, Muhammad married a further nine times in all, mostly to widows of companions who had lost their lives fighting the Quraysh. Muhammad made at least two political marriages: the first was to Maria, a Coptic slave girl, and the second to a Jewess who had been captured in battle. By far the most controversial of Muhammad's relationships were his marriages to Aisha, the daughter of his close companion Abu Bakr, and to Zaynab, the divorced wife of his adopted son Zayd. The marriage between Muhammad and Aisha was contracted when she was probably no more than ten years old: the sources do not mention her age directly, but say that when she went to live in the Prophet's house, she passed much of the time playing with her toys, and was often joined in her games by Muhammad himself.

A relationship between a man in his early fifties and a child often is bound to raise more than a few eyebrows today, particularly in Western cultural milieus where sensitivity regarding issues such as pedophilia is heightened. Unsurprisingly, one of the charges levelled against the Prophet by his detractors is that his relationship with Aisha was tantamount to child abuse. A marriage between an older man and a young girl was customary among the Bedouins, as it still is in many societies across the world today. It was not unheard of in Muhammad's time for boys and girls to be promised to each other in marriage almost as soon as they were born, particularly if the union was of direct political significance to the families concerned. However, such marriages were almost certainly not consummated until both parties had entered adulthood, which Arabs in the seventh century tended to reach at an earlier age than Westerners today. It is highly unlikely that Muhammad would not have taken Aisha into his bed until she was at least in her early teens, which was wholly in keeping with the customs of the day, and in context not in the least improper.

The Basics of Islam
Colin Turner
Durham University,
School of Government and International Affairs,
Faculty Member

There was no impropriety in Muhammad's betrothal to 'A'isha. Marriages conducted in absentia to seal an alliance were often contracted at this time between adults and minors who were even younger than 'A'isha. This practice continued in Europe well into the early modern period. There was no question of consummating the marriage until A'isha reached puberty, when she would have been married off like any other girl. Muhammad's marriages usually had a political aim. He was starting to establish an entirely different kind of clan, based on ideology rather than kinship, but the blood tie was still a sacred value and helped to cement this experimental community.

Muhammad: A Biography of the Prophet
Karen Armstrong
Author and Comparative Religion Scholar from Great Britain

A female also at seven years of age may be betrothed of given in marriage; at nine is entitled to dower; at twelve is at years of maturity, and therefore may consent or disagree to marriage, and, if proved to have sufficient discretion, may bequeath her personal estate; at fourteen is at years of discretion and may choose a guardian; at seventeen maybe executrix; and at twenty one may dispose of herself and her land.

William Blackstone
Commentaries of The laws of England
English Jurist, Judge and Tory Politician (1723-1780)

MONARCH MARRIAGES UNDER THE CATHOLIC CHURCH

Name: Petronilla of Aragon
Date of Birth: 29th June 1136
Age When Married: One
Religion: Roman Catholic

She was Queen of Aragon (1137–1164) from the abdication of her father, Ramiro II, in 1137 until her own abdication in 1164. After her abdication she acted as regent during the minority of her son Alfonso II of Aragon (1164–1173). She was the last ruling member of the Jiménez dynasty in Aragon, and by marriage brought the throne to the House of Barcelona.

Pope Innocent II rejected this election, seeking to affirm Alfonso I's final will. Despite the lack of papal approval, King Ramiro the Monk, as he is known, married Agnes of Aquitaine in 1135.

Petronilla's marriage was a very important matter of state. The nobility had rejected the proposition of Alfonso VII of Castile to arrange a marriage between Petronilla and his son Sancho and to educate her at his court. When she was just a little over one year old, Petronilla was betrothed in Barbastro on 11 August 1137 to Raymond Berengar IV, Count of Barcelona, who was twenty three years her senior.

Name: Bianca Maria Sforza
Date of Birth: 5th April 1472
Age When Married: Two
Religion: Roman Catholic

She was Queen of Germany and Empress of the Holy Roman Empire as the third spouse of Maximilian I. She was the eldest legitimate daughter of Duke Galeazzo Maria Sforza of Milan by his second wife, Bona of Savoy.

On 6th January 1474 the 21-month-old Bianca was betrothed to her first cousin Duke Philibert I of Savoy, the son of her uncle Amadeus IX of Savoy, and Yolande of France. Duke Philibert I died in the spring of 1482, leaving Bianca a widow at the age of ten. She returned to Milan, under the tutelage of her uncle Ludovico Il Moro, who cared little about her education and allowed her to indulge her own interests, mainly needlework.

Name: Margaret of France, Queen of England and Hungary
Date of Birth: 1158
Age When Married: Two
Religion: Roman Catholic

She was junior Queen of England by marriage to Henry the Young King until his death in 1183, and Queen of Hungary and Croatia by marriage to Bela III of Hungary from 1186.

Margaret was the eldest daughter of Louis VII of France by his second wife Constance of Castile. Her older half-sisters, Marie and Alix, were also older half-sisters of her future husband.

She was betrothed to Henry the Young King on 2nd November 1160. Henry was the second son of King Henry II of England and Eleanor of Aquitaine. He was five years old at the time of this agreement while Margaret was about two. Margaret's dowry was the vital and much disputed territory of Vexin.

Name: Marie de Bourbon, Duchess of Montpensier
Date of Birth: 15th October 1605
Age When Married: Two
Religion: Roman Catholic

Duchess of Montpensier, and Duchess of Orleans by marriage, was a French noblewoman and one of the last members of the House of Bourbon Montpensier. Her parents were Henri de Bourbon, Duke of Montpensier and Henriette Catherine de Joyeuse, Duchess of Joyeuse in her own right.

At the age of two, she had been engaged to the second son of Henry IV of France, Nicolas Henri de France, Duke of Orleans, but he died at the age of four in 1611. She was then betrothed to his brother, Gaston de France, Duke of Orleans, the younger brother of King Louis XIII, and the heir presumptive to the throne of France.

Name: Margaret III, Countess of Flanders
Date of Birth: 13th April 1350
Age When Married: Five
Religion: Roman Catholic

She was a ruling Countess of Flanders, Countess of Artois, and Countess of Auvergne and Boulogne between 1384 and 1405. She was the last Countess of Flanders of the House of Dampierre.

She was also Duchess of Burgundy by marriage to Philip I, Duke of Burgundy and Philip II, Duke of Burgundy.

In 1355, Margaret of Flanders married Philip of Rouvres, grandson and heir of Odo IV, Duke of Burgundy. Philip was Count of Burgundy and Artois (1347–1361), Duke of Burgundy (1350–1361), and became Count of Auvergne and Boulogne (1360–1361).

Name: Anne de Mowbray, 8th Countess of Norfolk
Date of Birth: 10th December 1472
Age When Married: Five
Religion: Roman Catholic

She later Duchess of York and Duchess of Norfolk (10th December 1472 – 19th November 1481) was the child bride of Richard of Shrewsbury, Duke of York, one of the Princes in the Tower.

On 15th January 1478, aged 5, she was married in St Stephen's Chapel, Westminster, to Richard of Shrewsbury, Duke of York, the 4 year old younger son of King Edward IV and his queen, Elizabeth Woodville.

Name: Joan II of Navarre
Date of Birth: 28th January 1312
Age When Married: Six
Religion: Roman Catholic

She was Queen of Navarre from 1328 until her death. She was the only surviving child of Louis X of France, King of France and Navarre, and Margaret of Burgundy.

Philip V was eventually pressured to renegotiate his niece's status. An agreement reached on 27th March 1318 included territorial concessions which placated Joan's maternal family, as well as her betrothal to Philip of Evreux, a dowry and a promise of succession to the counties of Champagne and Brie (also Joan I of Navarre's patrimony) if King Philip V were to die sonless.

Philip's marriage to Joan was celebrated on 18th June, after which she lived with his grandmother Queen Marie. A dispensation had been sought because Joan was only six years old. Although they lived near each other, Philip and Joan were not raised together due to age difference. Their union was not consummated until 1324.

Name: Isabella of Valois
Date of Birth: 9th November 1389
Age When Married: Seven
Religion: Roman Catholic

She was Queen of England as the wife of Richard II, King of England between 1396 and 1399, and Duchess of Orleans as the wife of Charles, Duke of Orleans from 1406 until her death in 1409. She had been born a princess of France as the daughter of King Charles VI and Isabeau of Bavaria.

In 1396 negotiations started about marrying six-year-old Isabella to the widower Richard II, King of England (1367–1400), who was 22 years her senior, to ensure peace between their countries. The fact that she was a child was discussed, but King Richard said that each day would rectify that problem; that it was an advantage as he would then be able to shape her in accordance with his ideal; and that he was young enough to wait. Isabella told the English envoys (who described her as pretty) that she was happy to be Queen of England as she had been told that this would make her a great lady. She also started practicing for the role.

Name: Maria of Navarre
Date of Birth: 1329
Age When Married: Seven
Religion: Roman Catholic

She was Queen of Aragon from 1338 until her death as the first of four wives of Peter IV of Aragon. The marriage contract was signed in her father's castle on Anet on 6th January 1336. It stipulated that, if her mother died leaving no sons, Maria or her children would inherit the crown of Navarre. The wedding ceremony took place near Zaragoza on 25th July 1337.

Name: Margaret of Bohemia, Queen of Hungary
Date of Birth: 24th May 1335
Age When Married: Seven
Religion: Roman Catholic

She also known as Margaret of Luxembourg, was a Queen consort of Hungary by her marriage to Louis I of Hungary. She was the second child of Charles IV, Holy Roman Emperor by his first wife Blanche of Valois. She was a member of the House of Luxembourg. Margaret was the second child of her father's first marriage. She was betrothed at the age of two to Amadeus VI, Count of Savoy, and the contract being signed on 7 March 1338. The contract was, however, broken and Amadeus married Margaret's cousin, Bonne of Bourbon. At the age of seven, Margaret was married in 1342 to Louis I of Hungary.

Name: Catherine of Savoy-Vaud
Date of Birth: 1324
Age When Married: Seven
Religion: Roman Catholic

She was an Italian vassal. She was suo jure Baron of Vaud in 1349 – 1359. In 1359, she sold the Barony to Amadeus VI, Count of Savoy, which united Vaud to Savoy. She was born to Louis II of Vaud and Isabelle, daughter of John I, lord of Arlay.

She married:

1. Azzone Visconti in 1331 (widowed in 1339); one daughter

2. Raoul II of Brienne, Count of Eu, in 1340 (widowed in 1350); no children

3. William I, Marquis of Namur, in 1352; three children.

Name: Anne of Gloucester
Date of Birth: 30th April 1383
Age When Married: Seven
Religion: Roman Catholic

She was the eldest daughter and eventually sole heiress of Thomas of Woodstock, 1st Duke of Gloucester (the fifth surviving son and youngest child of King Edward III), by his wife Eleanor de Bohun, one of the two daughters and co-heiresses of

Humphrey de Bohun, 7th Earl of Hereford, 6th Earl of Essex (1341–1373) of Pleshey Castle in Essex.

Anne married three times. Her first marriage was to Thomas Stafford, 3rd Earl of Stafford (1368 – 4th July 1392), and took place around 1390. The couple had no children. After her husband's death, Anne married his younger brother Edmund.

Name: Margaret I, Countess of Burgundy
Date of Birth: 1310
Age When Married: Seven
Religion: Roman Catholic

She was a Capetian princess who ruled as Countess of Burgundy and Artois from 1361 until her death. She was also countess of Flanders, Nevers and Rethel by marriage to Louis I of Flanders, and regent of Flanders during the minority of her son, Louis II, in 1346. Margaret's husband was killed in the Battle of Crecy on 26th August 1346. He and Margaret had one son, Count Louis II of Flanders, who succeeded his father and for whom she acted as a regent in the beginning of his reign.

In 1357, Margaret's granddaughter, Margaret, then seven years old, was married to Duke Philip I of Burgundy, grandson and heir of Margaret's sister. They were childless and, upon his death in 1361, the elder Margaret succeeded to the comital thrones of Artois and Burgundy.

Name: Marie of Brittany, Lady of La Guerche
Date of Birth: 18th February 1391
Age When Married: Five
Religion: Roman Catholic

She was the Countess of Perche and Lady of La Guerche from 1396 until 1414, and the Countess of Alencon from 1404 until 1414. In 1414, Marie's titles became Duchess of Alencon, Countess of Perche, Lady of La Guerche, when Charles VI of France raised her husband John's county of Alencon to a duchy. After the death of her husband in 1415, Marie retained the title of Lady of La Guerche when her son, John II took the titles of Duke of Alencon and Count of Perche. Marie was the link between the House of Montfort of the duchy of Brittany and the ducal House of Valois Alencon.

On 26th June 1396, John IV of Brittany signed a contract with Pierre of Alencon and Perche which wedded Marie of Brittany to John of Perche, Pierre's son. The wedding was celebrated in July of that year at Saint-Aubin-du-Cormier, Ille-et-Vilaine, near Fougeres. Marie's dowry was to be 100,000 francs, but her father never paid the entire amount, creating tension between the duchies of Brittany and Alencon in later years.

Name: Matilda of Hainaut
Date of Birth: November 1293
Age When Married: Seven
Religion: Roman Catholic

She also known as Maud and Mahaut, was Princess of Achaea from 1316 to 1321. She was the only child of Isabella of Villehardouin and Florent of Hainaut, co-rulers of Achaea 1289–1297. After Florent's death in 1297, Isabella continued to rule alone until she married to Guy II de la Roche in 1300. Guy II de la Roche was the Duke of Athens from 1287, the last duke of his family.

Name: Barbara of Brandenburg
Date of Birth: 30th May 1464
Age When Married: Eight
Religion: Roman Catholic

She was a member of the German House of Hohenzollern, was by birth Margravine of Brandenburg, and by her two marriages, Duchess of Głogow from 1472 to 1476, and Queen of Bohemia (although only nominally) from 1476 to 1490/1500.

In Berlin on 11th October 1472, eight year old Barbara was married to the Silesian Piast Duke Henry XI of Głogow, around thirty years her senior. The marriage contract stipulated that, in case of the duke's death without issue, his Duchy of Głogow was to be passed to his wife, with reversion to her Hohenzollern family.

Name: Elizabeth of Hungary, Duchess of Greater Poland
Date of Birth: 1128
Age When Married: Eight
Religion: Roman Catholic

She was a member of the House of Arpad and by marriage Duchess of Greater Poland. Around 1136, Elizabeth married with Prince Mieszko, son of the Polish ruler Bolesław III Wrymouth. The wedding was performed as a result of the agreement concluded a year earlier in Merseburg. Two years later (28th October 1138), Duke Bolesław III died; according to his will, Mieszko inherited the Greater Poland province and became in his first duke, with Elizabeth as his duchess.

Name: Elisabeth of Bohemia
Date of Birth: 1358
Age When Married: Eight
Religion: Roman Catholic

She was the daughter of Charles IV, Holy Roman Emperor, and Anne of Schweidnitz. She was named after her paternal grandmother, Elisabeth of Bohemia (1292–1330). Elisabeth married when she was only eight in 1366 to Albert III, Duke of Austria. Elisabeth and Albert had no children and she died aged only fifteen in 1373; she was buried with Albert's parents in Gaming Charterhouse in Lower Austria.

Name: Joanna I of Naples
Date of Birth: December 1325
Age When Married: Eight
Religion: Roman Catholic

Andrew was the second of three surviving sons of King Charles I of Hungary and his third wife, Elizabeth of Poland. He was betrothed in 1334 to his cousin Joanna, granddaughter and heiress apparent of King Robert of Naples; Andrew's father was a fraternal nephew of King Robert, making Andrew and Joanna both members of the Capetian House of Anjou. She married Andrew in 1333.

Name: Judith of Swabia
Date of Birth: 1054
Age When Married: Nine
Religion: Roman Catholic

She was a member of the Salian dynasty, was the youngest daughter of Emperor Henry III from his second marriage with Agnes of Poitou. By her two marriages she was Queen of Hungary from 1063 to 1074 and Duchess of Poland from 1089 to 1102. When King Andrew I died in 1060, his widow and sons had to take refuge in Germany. Nevertheless, with the support of his powerful brother-in-law, Solomon could recover the Hungarian throne after the death of his uncle Bela I in 1063 and soon after married with Judith in Szekesfehervar.

Alwy M. Jones

Name: Charlotte of Savoy
Date of Birth: 1443
Age When Married: Nine
Religion: Roman Catholic

She was the Queen of France as the second spouse of Louis XI. She served as regent during the king's absence in 1465, and was a member of the royal regency council during her son's minority in 1483.

On 11th March 1443, when Charlotte was just over a year old, she was betrothed to Frederick of Saxony (28th August 1439- 23rd December 1451), eldest son of Frederick II, Elector of Saxony. For reasons unknown, the betrothal was annulled. Less than eight years later on 14th February 1451, Charlotte married Louis, Dauphin of France (future Louis XI), eldest son of Charles VII of France and Marie of Anjou. The bride was nine years old and the groom twenty seven. The marriage, which had taken place without the consent of the French king, was Louis' second; his first spouse, Margaret of Scotland, had died childless in 1445. Upon her marriage, Charlotte became Dauphine of France.

Name: Anne de La Tour d'Auvergne
Date of Birth: 1496
Age When Married: Nine
Religion: Roman Catholic

She was the sovereign Countess of Auvergne from 1501 until 1524, and Duchess of Albany by marriage to John Stewart, Duke of Albany. In her marriage contract, she was called 'Anne de Boulogne fille de Jehan Comte de Boulogne et Auvergne. On 13th July 1505, she married her first cousin John Stewart, Duke of Albany, the intermittent heir presumptive to the Kingdom of Scotland and its sometime-regent, who lived in France as a sort of exile.

Name: Joan, Countess of Toulouse
Date of Birth: 1220
Age When Married: Nine
Religion: Roman Catholic

She was the Countess of Toulouse from 1249 until her death. She was the only child of Raymond VII, Count of Toulouse by his first wife Sancha of Aragon.

Joan was born at the Castle of Corneto near Siena. In 1225, aged five, Joan was betrothed to Hugh, eldest son and heir of Hugh X of Lusignan and Isabella, Countess of Angouleme and Dowager Queen of England. However, the engagement was soon broken.

One of the conditions of the Treaty of Paris, signed on 12th April 1229, stipulated that Joan was to be married to Alphonse, Count of Poitiers and brother of King Louis IX of France, and a Papal dispensation for their 4th degree of consanguinity is dated on 26th June of that year.

Name: Marie, Countess of Ponthieu
Date of Birth: 17th April 1199
Age When Married: Nine
Religion: Roman Catholic

She was suo jure Countess of Ponthieu and Countess of Montreuil, ruling from 1221 to 1250. She married Simon of Dammartin before September 1208. He was the son of Alberic II of Dammartin and Maud de Clermont, daughter of Renaud de Clermont, Count de Clermont-en-Beauvaisis. Simon and Marie had four daughters but only two are recorded.

Name: Alys of France, Countess of Vexin
Date of Birth: 4th October 1160
Age When Married: Eight
Religion: Roman Catholic

Also known in English as "Alice", was a French princess, the daughter of Louis VII, King of France and his second wife, Constance of Castile.

In January 1169, Louis and King Henry II of England signed a contract for the marriage between Alys and Henry's son Richard the Lionheart. The 8 year old Alys was then sent to England as Henry's ward.

In 1177, Cardinal Peter of Saint Chrysogonus, on behalf of Pope Alexander III, threatened to place England's continental possessions under an interdict if Henry did not proceed with the marriage. There were widespread rumors that Henry had not only made Alys his mistress, but that she had a child with him.

Name: Sidonie of Podebrady
Date of Birth: 11th November 1449
Age When Married: Ten
Religion: Roman Catholic

She was a duchess consort of Saxony. She was a daughter of George of Podebrady, King of Bohemia, and his first wife Kunigunde of Sternberg. She was the twin sister of Catherine of Podebrady, wife of Matthias Corvinus of Hungary.

A marriage contract was signed on 11th November 1459 for Sidonie's marriage to Albert, son of Frederick II, Elector of Saxony. The couple married on 11th May 1464. Sidonie followed her husband to Meissen, and the consummation of their marriage took place in May 1464 at Castle Tharandt.

Name: Catherine of Vendome
Date of Birth: 1354
Age When Married: Ten
Religion: Roman Catholic

She was a ruling countess of Vendome and of Castres from 1372 until 1403. Catherine was the daughter of John VI of Vendome and Jeanne of Ponthieu. She married John I, Count of La Marche, in 1364.

Name: Isabella of Aragon, Queen of Germany
Date of Birth: 1305
Age When Married: Ten
Religion: Roman Catholic

She was the daughter of James II of Aragon and his second wife Blanche of Anjou. The queen consort of Frederick I of Austria, she was a member of the House of Barcelona. On 11th May 1315, Isabella married Frederick I of Austria, King of Germany in Ravensburg.

Name: Anne of Auvergne
Date of Birth: 1358
Age When Married: Ten
Religion: Roman Catholic

She was Sovereign Dauphine of Auvergne 1400-1417 and Countess of Forez in 1372-1417 as well as Dame de Mercoeur from 1400 and 1417. She was also Duchess of Bourbon by marriage to Louis II, Duke of Bourbon.

Anne was betrothed to her cousin Louis when she was ten years old. The marriage contract was signed at Montbrison on 4th July 1368 and the pair were married in person at Ardes in January 1370. Due to the fact that the couple were cousins, a papal dispensation was required; this was granted to them by the Pope on 15th September 1370.

Name: Blanche of Brittany
Date of Birth: 1271
Age When Married: Ten
Religion: Roman Catholic

She was a daughter of John II, Duke of Brittany, and his wife Beatrice of England. She is also known as Blanche de Dreux. Through her mother she was the granddaughter of King Henry III of England and Eleanor of Provence. Blanche was married in Paris sometime after November 1281 to Philip of Artois, who was the son of Robert II of Artois and Amice de Courtenay.

Name: Joan III, Countess of Burgundy
Date of Birth: 2nd May 1308
Age When Married: Ten
Religion: Roman Catholic

She was also known as Joan of France was a reigning Countess of Burgundy and Artois in 1330–1347. She was also Duchess of Burgundy by marriage to Odo IV, Duke of Burgundy. Joan was the eldest daughter of King Philip V of France and Countess Joan II of Burgundy. She was married in 1318 to Odo IV, Duke of Burgundy, as part of a settlement between the two men regarding the French succession (Odo had previously supported the right of his niece and Joan's cousin - Queen Joan II of Navarre, to inherit the French throne as well); Joan thus became Duchess consort of Burgundy by marriage.

Name: Joan, Countess of Blois
Date of Birth: 1253
Age When Married: Ten
Religion: Roman Catholic

She was Countess of Blois from 1280 to 1291, and Lady of Avesnes. In 1263, Joanne married Peter of Alençon, a son of King Louis IX of France and Margaret of Provence.

Name: Margaret II, Countess of Flanders
Date of Birth: 1202
Age When Married: Ten
Religion: Roman Catholic

Often called Margaret of Constantinople (1202 – 10 February 1280), ruled as Countess of Flanders during 1244–1278 and Countess of Hainaut during 1244–1253 and 1257–1280. She was the younger daughter of Baldwin IX, Count of Flanders and Hainaut, and Marie of Champagne.

After her sister's marriage with Infante Ferdinand of Portugal, Margaret was placed under the care of Bouchard of Avesnes, Lord of Etroen and a prominent Hainaut nobleman, who was knighted by Baldwin IX before he parted to the Crusades. In the middle of the war against France for the possession of the Artois and the forced territorial concession made by the Treaty of Pont-a-Vendin, Joan and Ferdinand wanted to marry Margaret with William II Longespee, heir of the Earldom of Salisbury, in order to reinforce the bonds of Flanders with England; however Bouchard of Avesnes, with the consent of the King of France, prevented the union.

Despite the considerable age difference between them, Bouchard gained Margaret's affection, and in the presence of a significant number of bourgeois of Hainaut, she declared she did not want another husband than him, and before 23rd July 1212 they were married.

Name: Mariana Victoria of Spain
Date of Birth: 31st March 1718
Age When Married: Eleven
Religion: Roman Catholic

She was an Infanta of Spain by birth and was later the Queen of Portugal as wife of King Joseph I. She acted as regent of Portugal in 1776–1777, during the last months of her husband's life and as advisor to her daughter, Maria I of Portugal, in her reign.

Mariana Victoria married the Prince of Brazil (traditional title for the Portuguese heir to the throne) on 19th January 1729 at Elvas in Portugal. The Prince of Asturias (traditional title for the Spanish heir to the throne) married the Infanta Bárbara the next day at Badajoz. From her marriage until the time of her husband's accession to the throne in 1750, she was styled Her Royal Highness the Princess of Brazil.

Name: Philippa of England
Date of Birth: 1394
Age When Married: Eleven
Religion: Roman Catholic

She also known as Philippa of Lancaster, was Queen of Denmark, Norway and Sweden from 1406 to 1430 by marriage to King Eric of the Kalmar Union. She was the daughter of King Henry IV of England by his first spouse Mary de Bohun and the younger sister of King Henry V. Queen Philippa participated significantly in state affairs during the reign of her spouse, and served as regent of Denmark from 1423 to 1425.

Queen Margaret could not agree to the terms and the marriage between Henry and Catherine never occurred. In 1405, however, a Scandinavian embassy composed of two envoys from each of the three Nordic kingdoms arrived in England, and the marriage between Philippa and Eric was proclaimed. On 26th November 1405, Philippa was married to Eric by proxy in Westminster, with the Swedish nobleman Ture Bengtsson Bielke as the stand-in for the groom, and on 8 December, she was formally proclaimed Queen of Denmark, Norway and Sweden in the presence of the Nordic ambassadors.

Name: Louise of Savoy
Date of Birth: 11th September 1476
Age When Married: Eleven
Religion: Roman Catholic

She was a French noble and regent, Duchess suo jure of Auvergne and Bourbon, Duchess of Nemours and the mother of King Francis I and Marguerite of Navarre. She was politically active and served as the regent of France in 1515, in 1525–1526 and in 1529, during the absence of her son.

At age eleven, Louise married Charles of Orleans, Count of Angouleme, on 16th February 1488 in Paris.

She only began living with him when she was fifteen, though. Despite her husband having two mistresses, the marriage was not unhappy and they shared a love for books.

Name: Anne Lascaris
Date of Birth: November 1487
Age When Married: Eleven
Religion: Roman Catholic

She countess of Tende and of Villars, was a French noblewoman. She was the daughter of Jean-Antoine II de Lascaris, comte de Tende and Ventimiglia, lord of Mentone, and his wife Isabeau (or Isabelle) d'Anglure-Estoges.

At 11 and a half years old, Anne married Louis de Clermont-Lodeve, vicomte de Nebousan.

Name: Ermesinde, Countess of Luxembourg
Date of Birth: July 1186
Age When Married: Eleven
Religion: Roman Catholic

She ruled as the countess of Luxembourg from 1197 until her death. She was the only child of Count Henry IV and his second wife Agnes of Guelders.

Ermesinde was initially betrothed to Count Henry II of Champagne, but the engagement was cancelled in 1189. Instead her first husband was Count Theobald I of Bar. They married in 1197.

Name: Isabella I of Jerusalem
Date of Birth: 1172
Age When Married: Eleven
Religion: Roman Catholic

She was reigning Queen of Jerusalem from 1190 to her death in 1205. She was the daughter of Amalric I of Jerusalem and his second wife Maria Comnena, a Byzantine princess.

The wedding took place in Kerak Castle. Saladin, the Ayyubid sultan of Egypt and Syria laid siege to the fortress. She married Humphrey IV of Toron in 1183.

Name: Joan I of Navarre
Date of Birth: 14th January 1273
Age When Married: Eleven
Religion: Roman Catholic

She was ruling Queen of Navarre and Countess of Champagne from 1274 until 1305. She was also Queen of France by marriage to King Philip IV. She founded the College of Navarre in Paris in 1305.

At the age of 11, Joan married the future Philip IV of France on 16th August 1284, becoming queen consort of France in 1285 a year later. Their three surviving sons would all rule as kings of France, in turn, and their only surviving daughter, Isabella, became queen consort of England.

Name: Judith of Flanders
Date of Birth: 844
Age When Married: Twelve
Religion: Roman Catholic

She was a Carolingian princess who became Queen of Wessex by two successive marriages and later Countess of Flanders. In 855, the widower Ethelwulf, King of Wessex (died 858) made a pilgrimage to Rome with his youngest son Alfred (848/849–899). On the way there, he visited the court of Charles the Bald and negotiated for a marriage with 12 year old Judith, despite probably being in his mid-fifties and having six children, three or five of them older than Judith. He was looking for an ally as both he and Charles suffered from Viking attacks. Marrying into the prestigious Carolingian dynasty was an additional advantage for Ethelwulf.

Name: Isabella of Angouleme
Date of Birth: 1188
Age When Married: Twelve
Religion: Roman Catholic

She was Queen of England from 1200 to 1216 as the second wife of King John, Countess of Angouleme in her own right from 1202 until her death in 1246, and Countess of La Marche from 1220 to 1246 as the wife of Count Hugh. Isabella became Countess of Angouleme in her own right on 16th June 1202, by which time she was already queen of England. Her marriage, at age 12 to King John took place on 24th August 1200, in Angouleme, a year after he annulled his first marriage to Isabel of Gloucester.

Name: Agnes of Navarre
Date of Birth: 1337
Age When Married: Twelve
Religion: Roman Catholic

She was the daughter of Philip III of Navarre and Joan II of Navarre, and became Countess of Foix on marriage to Gaston III, Count of Foix. She was rumoured to have had an affair with poet Guillaume de Machaut and so inspired his poem Le Voir Dit. In 1349, Agnes married Gaston Febus, Count of Foix. This was a strategic marriage, as the counts of Foix were neighbors who had provided military support in a 1335 war between Navarre and Castile.

Name: Viacheslava of Novgorod
Date of Birth: 1125
Age When Married: Twelve
Religion: Roman Catholic

She was a Kievan Rus' princess member of the Monomakhovichi and by marriage Duchess of Masovia and Kuyavia and High Duchess of Poland since 1146.

Around 1137 she was married to Bolesław, son of the Polish Duke Bolesław III Wrymouth. The wedding was probably orchestrated by Bolesław's mother Salomea of Berg, who wanted to secure a Russian alliance against her stepson, the later Władysław II the Exile.

Name: Hedwig of Silesia
Date of Birth: 1174
Age When Married: Twelve
Religion: Roman Catholic

She a member of the Bavarian comital House of Andechs, was Duchess of Silesia from 1201 and of Greater Poland from 1231 as well as High Duchess consort of Poland from 1232 until 1238. She was canonized by the Catholic Church in 1267 by Pope Clement IV.

At the age of twelve, Hedwig married Henry I the Bearded, son and heir of the Piast duke Boleslaus the Tall of Silesia.

Name: Anne of Bohemia, Duchess of Silesia
Date of Birth: 1204
Age When Married: Twelve
Religion: Roman Catholic

She was a member of the Premyslid dynasty, was Duchess of Silesia and High Duchess of Poland from 1238 to 1241, by her marriage to the Piast ruler Henry II the Pious. She was celebrated by the community of Franciscan nuns at St Clara of Prague Abbey in Wrocław as their founder and patron. Around the age of twelve (in 1216) she was married to the Piast prince Henry II the Pious, member of the Silesian branch of the Piast dynasty, the son and heir of Duke Henry the Bearded.

Name: Joanna of Bourbon
Date of Birth: 3rd February 1338
Age When Married: Twelve
Religion: Roman Catholic

She was Queen of France by marriage to King Charles V. She acted as his political adviser and was appointed potential regent in case of a minor regency. On 8th April 1350, Joanna married her cousin, the future Charles V of France, at Tain-l'Hermitage. Since they were first cousins once removed, their marriage required a papal dispensation. Born thirteen days apart, they both were 12 years old. When Charles ascended the throne in 1364, Joanna became queen of France.

Name: Margaret Stewart, Dauphine of France
Date of Birth: 25th December 1424
Age When Married: Twelve
Religion: Roman Catholic

She was a princess of Scotland and the dauphine of France. She was the firstborn child of King James I of Scotland and Joan Beaufort. Margaret was Charles VII of France's diplomatic choice for daughter-in-law. The marriage was forced upon Charles's twelve year old son, Louis, which did not help their relationship. It is universally agreed that Louis entered the ceremony and the marriage itself dutifully, as evidenced by his formal embrace of Margaret upon their first meeting on 24th June 1436, the day before their wedding.

Name: Margaret Holland, Duchess of Clarence
Date of Birth: 1385
Age When Married: Twelve
Religion: Roman Catholic

She was a medieval English noblewoman. She was a daughter of Thomas Holland, 2nd Earl of Kent, who was the son of Joan "the Fair Maid of Kent" (granddaughter of Edward I of England, wife of Edward the Black Prince and mother of Richard II of England). Margaret's mother was Alice Fitz Alan, daughter of Richard Fitz Alan, 10th Earl of Arundel and Eleanor of Lancaster.

Margaret married John Beaufort, 1st Earl of Somerset, son of John of Gaunt and his mistress Katherine Swynford in 1397.

Name: Eleanor of Lancaster
Date of Birth: 11th September 1318
Age When Married: Twelve
Religion: Roman Catholic

She was the fifth daughter of Henry, 3rd Earl of Lancaster and Maud Chaworth. Eleanor married first on 6th November 1330 John de Beaumont, 2nd Baron Beaumont (d. 1342), son of Henry Beaumont, 4th Earl of Buchan, 1st Baron Beaumont (c.1288-1340) by his wife Alice Comyn (1289-3rd July 1349). He died in a tournament on 14th April 1342.

Name: Gertrude of Supplingenburg
Date of Birth: 18th April 1115
Age When Married: Twelve
Religion: Roman Catholic

She was Duchess of Bavaria, Margravine of Tuscany, and Duchess of Saxony by marriage to Henry X, Duke of Bavaria, and Margravine of Austria and Duchess of Bavaria by marriage to Henry II, Duke of Austria. She was regent of Saxony during the minority of her son Henry the Lion in 1139–1142. Gertrude was married to Henry the Proud, Duke of Bavaria, a dynastic arrangement meant to strengthen ties to the Welf dynasty. The lavish wedding ceremony was held on 29th May 1127 on the Lech fields near Augsburg.

Name: Elisabeth of Carinthia, Queen of the Romans
Date of Birth: 1262
Age When Married: Twelve
Religion: Roman Catholic

She was a Duchess of Austria from 1282 and Queen of the Romans from 1298 until 1308, by marriage to King Albert I of Habsburg. Elisabeth was married in Vienna on 20th December 1274 to Count Albert I of Habsburg, eldest son and heir of the newly elected Rudolf I, King of the Romans, thus becoming daughter-in-law of the King of the Romans and Emperor to be.

Name: Adelasia of Torres
Date of Birth: 1207
Age When Married: Twelve
Religion: Roman Catholic

She was the Judge of Logudoro from 1236 and the titular Judge of Gallura from 1238. By a pact signed between her father, who had interests in Gallura, and Gallurese judge, the Pisan Lamberto Visconti in November 1218, Adelasia first married the heir of Gallura, Lamberto's son Ubaldo II in 1219. Pope Honorius III, enemy of the Pisans, immediately sent his chaplain Bartolomeo to annul the marriage, but he failed and the pact between Pisa and Logudoro stood.

Name: Anne Scott, 1st Duchess of Buccleuch
Date of Birth: 11th February 1651
Age When Married: Twelve
Religion: Roman Catholic

She was a wealthy Scottish peeress. After her father died when she was a few months old, and her sisters by the time she was 10, she inherited the family's titles. She was married to James Scott, 1st Duke of Monmouth, and the couple had six children, only two of whom survived past infancy. Upon her marriage in 1663, her husband took her surname, and the titles of Duke of Monmouth, Lord Scott of Whitchester and Eskdaill, Earl of Dalkeith, and Duke of Buccleuch were created, with remainder to the heirs male of his body by Anne, failing whom to the heirs whomsoever of her body who shall succeed to the estates and Earldom of Buccleuch.

Name: Catherine of Cleves
Date of Birth: 1548
Age When Married: Twelve
Religion: Roman Catholic

She was the wife of Henry I, Duke of Guise and the matriarch of the powerful and influential House of Guise. By marriage, she was Duchess of Guise from 1570 to 1588, and Dowager Duchess of Guise thereafter. At the age of twelve, Catherine married the 19 year old Antoine III de Croy, Prince de Porcien (or Porcean), who died seven years later, leaving her a widow at the young age of 19.

Name: Henriette Catherine de Joyeuse
Date of Birth: 8th January 1585
Age When Married: Twelve
Religion: Roman Catholic

She duchess of Joyeuse, de Montpensier and de Guise, countess of Eu and princess of Joinville is a French aristocrat, grandmother of the Great Miss.

On 15th may 1597, Henriette Catherine married Henri Bourbon, duke of Montpensier while she has only 13 Years, she was entrusted for a few years to her uncle, the cardinal Francois de Joyeuse.

Name: Isabella, Countess of Vertus
Date of Birth: 1st October 1348
Age When Married: Twelve
Religion: Roman Catholic

She was a French princess and member of the House of Valois, as well as the wife of Gian Galeazzo Visconti, who after her death became Duke of Milan. Her maternal uncle Count Amadeus VI of Savoy arranged her marriage with Gian Galeazzo Visconti. As her dowry, Isabella received the county of Sommieres, exchanged later for the county of Vertus. On 8th October 1360, Isabella and Gian Galeazzo were married in Milan, and six months later, in April 1361, she was declared sovereign Countess of Vertus.

Name: Maria Angelina Doukaina Palaiologina
Date of Birth: 1351
Age When Married: Ten
Religion: Roman Catholic

She was a Byzantine Greek-Serbian aristocrat and the self-proclaimed basilissa of Epirus from 1384–85, succeeding the rule of her murdered husband Thomas Preljubovic. Maria and her husband were a famed couple as patrons of the arts during Tomo's rule of Ioannina from 1366 to 1384. Her maternal grandfather was John Orsini of Epirus. In 1361, Maria, then only 10 years old, married Thomas Preljubovic, who was appointed the governor (despot) of Epirus in Ioannina by her father in 1366.

Name: Agnes of Waiblingen
Date of Birth: 1072
Age When Married: Fourteen
Religion: Roman Catholic

She was also known as Agnes of Germany, Agnes of Franconia and Agnes of Saarbrücken, was a member of the Salian imperial family. Through her first marriage, she was Duchess of Swabia; through her second marriage, she was Margravine of Austria.

In 1079, aged seven, Agnes was betrothed to Frederick, a member of the Hohenstaufen dynasty; at the same time, Henry IV invested Frederick as the new duke of Swabia. The couple married in 1086, when Agnes was fourteen.

Alwy M. Jones

Telegram

WhatsApp

Alwy M. Jones

YouTube

Buy Me Coffee

Milton Keynes UK
Ingram Content Group UK Ltd.
UKHW041821201024
449814UK00001B/45